NO TIME
FOR
TACT

365 DAYS OF THE WIT, WORDS, AND WISDOM OF LARRY WINGET

LARRY WINGET

NO TIME
FOR
TACT

GOTHAM
BOOKS

GOTHAM BOOKS
Published by Penguin Group (USA) Inc.
375 Hudson Street, New York, New York 10014, U.S.A.
Penguin Group (Canada), 90 Eglinton Avenue East, Suite 700, Toronto, Ontario
M4P 2Y3, Canada (a division of Pearson Penguin Canada Inc.); Penguin Books
Ltd, 80 Strand, London WC2R 0RL, England; Penguin Ireland, 25 St Stephen's
Green, Dublin 2, Ireland (a division of Penguin Books Ltd); Penguin Group
(Australia), 250 Camberwell Road, Camberwell, Victoria 3124, Australia (a
division of Pearson Australia Group Pty Ltd); Penguin Books India Pvt Ltd,
11 Community Centre, Panchsheel Park, New Delhi—110 017, India; Penguin
Group (NZ), 67 Apollo Drive, Rosedale, North Shore 0632, New Zealand (a
division of Pearson New Zealand Ltd); Penguin Books (South Africa) (Pty)
Ltd, 24 Sturdee Avenue, Rosebank, Johannesburg 2196, South Africa

Penguin Books Ltd, Registered Offices: 80 Strand, London WC2R 0RL, England

Published by Gotham Books, a member of Penguin Group (USA) Inc.

First printing, September 2009

10 9 8 7 6 5 4 3 2 1

LIBRARY OF CONGRESS CATALOGING-IN-PUBLICATION DATA
Winget, Larry.
    No time for tact: 365 days of the wit, words, and wisdom of Larry Winget /
by Larry Winget.
        p. cm
    ISBN 978-1-592-40503-9
1. Self-help techniques—Humor. I. Title.
    BF632.W56 2009
    081—dc22   2009009300

Printed in the United States of America

Set in Olympian LT Std • Designed by Sabrina Bowers

A NOTE FROM LARRY

This is my favorite type of book. No kidding. I own dozens of books from a variety of authors that are similar to this one. That's why I am so happy that I am having one of my own published and I am happy that it's in your hands right now. I love books that have one thought per page. I also love books that cover a variety of topics. I love books that have daily readings, sometimes giving me only one great line per day and sometimes giving me a longer observation or thought. I like good, solid content some days. Other days, I want something that just makes me laugh. Mostly, I like stuff that makes me think, that makes me want to call a buddy and say, "Hey, you gotta hear this!"

I also like this book because I would consider it a true "Best of Larry." These pages are full of ideas, quotations, and passages from all of my other books. If you aren't familiar with my other books, these little snippets are designed to let you get a feel for who I am. If you like these short thoughts, observations, rants, and ideas, you can go to any of my other books for more information because now you know who I am, what I believe, how I write, and what I am all about. For my seasoned readers, this is my philosophy distilled. Think back on all the advice I have given you in my past books. Now you have no excuse not to follow it because I'm going to be with you for a page a day, every day, for an entire year.

What I like best about this book is that it has a little bit of everything for everyone, regardless of what you are looking for.

Whether you decide to read this book a day at a time or devour it all at once, I know the first thing each of you will do is go to your birthday and see what I said on "your" day. That's how people are. We always relate information to ourselves. Actually, that is exactly how I want you to use this book. Think about what I have to say, and then think about how what I have said applies to you and your life. If you think something I have said will work for you, then give it a try. If what I say on a particular day doesn't work for you, the good news is that there are 364 more thoughts you might be able to use. Even if you find only one good idea in here that you can use to change your life in a positive way, this book will have been worth the read.

Enjoy!

LARRY WINGET

(Now, go to your birthday! I hope I said something good for you!)

JANUARY
1

Last year is over. Be done with it. Good or bad, it's over now. The past has passed.

Maybe you had some good things happen last year—I'm happy for you. Now it's time to go out and make some new good things happen.

Maybe you had some bad things happen. Oh, well, welcome to life; better luck next time.

It's a new year! Learn from your mistakes and move on!

JANUARY
2

Expect the best.

Be prepared for the worst.

Celebrate it all!

JANUARY
3

Someone sent me this question in an e-mail recently: "Larry, do you consider yourself an expert?"

Absolutely! However, I am not an expert on leadership, though I have led many successful organizations. I have led some into stardom and one into bankruptcy. Which one taught me the most? The one I led into bankruptcy.

I am not an expert at customer service. I have delivered both great and horrible service. I recognize it when I get both too. I am certainly not an expert at selling, though I have been an award-winning salesperson. I am not an expert at money or financial success, though I have gone from being bankrupt to being a multimillionaire. I am certainly not an expert at relationships; I have screwed up many of them. I have messed up in my marriage and with my kids numerous times.

All I am really an expert at is being stupid and learning from it. In fact, I could be the poster child for stupidity. The key is that I learn from my stupidity. I pay attention to my mistakes. I have become an expert at not making the same mistake twice and at learning from every stupid thing I have ever done. And I've become an expert at telling others how to learn from their mistakes.

I am not pretending to be something I am not, and I am not saying I am better than any of the others who write books and give speeches. I make more mistakes before noon than most people make in a month. But I do my best to learn from every stupid mistake I make. Try this approach yourself. Don't be afraid of making mistakes. Become an expert at learning from them.

JANUARY
4

Fight fair.

When you're having a fight, a disagreement, or an argument, stick to the issue—don't make it personal. Making it personal is not fair. Don't dredge up things from the past that have nothing to do with the issue. That's not fair either. Keep the fight about the subject at hand. Fights happen in the best of marriages and are a big part of a healthy relationship. You need to be able to disagree openly when you have differing opinions. People who say that they never fight with their spouse don't have much of a marriage.

JANUARY
5

If you are unhappy, unsuccessful, sick, or broke—please keep it to yourself. The rest of us do not want to hear about it, so don't feel compelled to share!

JANUARY
6

People are selfish. Understand it, deal with it, and manage it as best you can.

Don't be naive and pretend you don't understand it. You will only get hurt.

JANUARY
7

If a person does stupid things, he will get stupid results.

If a person does intelligent things, his results will reflect his behavior.

So which are you? Look at your results and you will know.

JANUARY
8

Training is expensive. Books are expensive. Going to seminars is expensive. All learning is expensive.

Being stupid is still much more expensive.

(Happy Birthday, Elvis!)

JANUARY
9

When you mess up, big deal. **Just admit it, fix it, and move on.** Other than that, life's a party!

—TYLER WINGET

JANUARY
10

Not all problems can be fixed. Don't kill yourself trying.

Sometimes your only choice is to learn to live with the problem. You have to work with the problem. Go around the problem. Move faster than the problem. Be smarter than the problem.

You can't avoid it; you just learn to deal with it.

JANUARY
11

Few people will turn to themselves to take responsibility for their results until they have exhausted all opportunities to blame someone else.

JANUARY
12

Both **business and life are a lot like golf.**
It's not so much about hitting the right shot every time; it's more about being able to correct a mishit.

JANUARY
13

The more successful you become, the fewer true friends you will have.

Why? Because while everyone you know wants you to be successful, they don't want you to be more successful than they are.

JANUARY
14

Lying is a character flaw. It destroys trust. It doesn't matter how small the lie is. **A lie is a lie is a lie.**
   A person who will lie about the small things will also lie about the big things.

JANUARY
15

When you hear the words **"I'll try,"**
you can bet your money it won't happen.

JANUARY
16

As a business owner or manager, ask yourself this question: **What do I pay my people for?**

The answer: results. Not time. Not attitude. Not enthusiasm or passion. Just results.

$$$$$$$$$$$$$$$

JANUARY
17

If you aren't willing to put your money
where your mouth is, you don't really be-
lieve in what you are doing.

$$$$$$$$$$$$$$$

JANUARY
18

There is no such thing as giving 110 percent. **One hundred percent is all there is—** you can't give more than all there is; that is why it's called all there is!

JANUARY
19

Most people will pay little attention to what you have to say.

Most won't even believe what you have to say.

They will, however, pay attention to see if *you* believe what you have to say.

JANUARY
20

Ready—willing—able.

Have you heard of those three? Of
course you have.

How many people are ready to be more
successful? Everyone. How many people
are able to be more successful? Everyone.
How many people are willing to do whatever it takes to become more successful?
Very few.

JANUARY
21

Sometimes you lose. When it happens, don't be a jerk about it. Then again, **sometimes you win.** When it happens, don't be a jerk about it.

JANUARY
22

People make changes when they want to make changes, not when **you** want them to and usually not when they need to.

JANUARY
23

Inspect what you expect.
Stuff doesn't happen just because you expect
it to happen; you have to make sure it happens
by inspecting the progress.

JANUARY
24

You always need a Plan B,

except when you don't have one.

In that case, you have to make the only plan you have work.

JANUARY
25

When you screw up:

Admit it,
make amends as best you can,
and then get back to work.

JANUARY
26

There are medical breakthroughs. There are scientific breakthroughs. There are no personal-development breakthroughs. **There is no brand-new stuff.**

No one is coming up with any brand-new keys to success. It's not going to happen. The people who tell you otherwise are playing on your weaknesses; they know you are thinking that the old stuff hasn't worked for you so far, so maybe something new will. Then they repackage the old stuff and call it new and improved in order to sucker you into buying it.

Go back to the old stuff, the stuff that has worked forever—stuff like taking responsibility, having integrity, being honest, and working hard. Those things will carry you as far as you will ever want to go.

JANUARY
27

The best advertisement in the whole world is a satisfied customer with a big mouth.

The worst advertisement in the whole world is an unsatisfied customer with a big mouth.

JANUARY
28

Don't worry too much about making the right decision.
Just make the decision,
and then make the decision right.

JANUARY
29

Knowledge is not power;
the implementation of knowledge is power.

$$$$$$$$$$$$$$$

JANUARY
30

Pay your taxes first, yourself second, and everyone else after that.

$$$$$$$$$$$$$$$

JANUARY
31

Drink in moderation.

A glass or two of wine has been proven to be beneficial for your health. For those of you who don't believe in drinking at all—rather than judge those of us who do, keep it to yourself and just choose not to drink. If you do drink, don't drink until you get drunk. You may think you are funny, but the rest of us just find you annoying. And the older you get, the longer it takes to recuperate.

FEBRUARY
1

It is impossible to grow without **pain** and without **risk.**

FEBRUARY
2

Kids do what they do because their parents allow them to do it. Kids become what they become because that is what their parents allow them to become. It's that simple. Now, if you are a parent with kids who have made a mess of their lives, you aren't going to like that answer. You are going to come back at me with a ton of excuses. You are going to talk about movies and music and sex and violence on television. You are going to blame the educational system. Trust me; I have heard it all before. I have watched parents say it all on television. I have even said some of it myself a time or two. But shake off your indignation and realize this basic truth: **Your kids are a product of your parenting.** Period. Deal with it. Now.

FEBRUARY
3

We will do damn near anything to keep from having to accept that we are the cause of our lives being the way they are.

We turn on our televisions and are seduced into victimhood by the reports we see on the news. Obviously the credit-card companies, mortgage companies, banks, oil companies, grocery stores, and retailers are the reasons we are broke and unsuccessful. We listen to the radio and hear the bankruptcy attorneys say they can rescue us because our financial situation is not our fault at all. Our friends tell us it is a cold, cruel world out there and it's no wonder we are having problems. It is so soothing to hear from any source that your pitiful life isn't your own fault . . . and there is the seduction.

We cling to the idea that maybe it is someone else's fault that we are unhappy, unsuccessful, sick, and broke. Please let it be someone else's fault! Please!

FEBRUARY
4

Praise in public and criticize in private.

That is a good rule for dealing with your employees, your friends, and your kids.

FEBRUARY
5

Don't think too much about how you are going to achieve your goals. **Too much analysis leads to paralysis.** Too much thought can create worry, and worry fosters fear and doubt. Don't be overly concerned with how you are going to get it all done. Just get started and learn as you go. Action creates courage, and momentum keeps you going.

FEBRUARY
6

Everything has a price.

Success has a price, and so does failure.

Choose either, but be prepared to pay the price for your choice.

FEBRUARY
7

Some days you must put up with the 90 percent of your job that you hate in order to get to the 10 percent of your job that you love.

FEBRUARY
8

Manage priorities, not time.

FEBRUARY
9

Here is what the credo of every business should be:

This is a sacred place where we only speak well of ourselves, we only speak well of our organization, we only speak well of our competitors, and we only speak well of our customers.

FEBRUARY
10

Larry's Ultimate Key for Success:

Discover your uniqueness and learn to exploit it in the service of others, and you are guaranteed success, happiness, and prosperity.

FEBRUARY
11

You destroy the **competition** when
you stop believing in it.

FEBRUARY
12

You don't have to love your job in order to be successful—but it helps.

You don't have to be passionate about your job in order to be successful—but it helps.

You don't have to be enthusiastic about your job in order to be successful—but it helps.

The real key to being successful in your job is excellence and hard work.

FEBRUARY
13

Results are everything, and **results never lie.**

$$$$$$$$$$$$$$

FEBRUARY
14

The average fifty-year-old in America has **less than $2,500 saved.**

Let's say you started working at age twenty-five, and you are now fifty years old. In twenty-five years you have managed to save only $2,500?

The best you could do was $100 per year?

All you could manage to put away was $8.33 per month?

You just couldn't seem to do much better than $2 per week?

Dear Mr. or Mrs. Average Fifty-Year-Old, **you are an idiot!**

$$$$$$$$$$$$$$

FEBRUARY
15

When you **expect** the work to get done quickly and you **reward** the work that is done quickly, the work will get done quickly.

FEBRUARY
16

People love to be sold and **hate to be hustled.** Sell with courtesy. Sell with common sense. Sell with tact. Don't push. Be sensitive. Back off when it feels like you should. Care enough about your customers to use your head, your ears, your eyes, your brain, and your heart to serve them well.

FEBRUARY
17

If you don't like your life the way it is, there is only one place to go when you are ready to lay the blame: the mirror.

FEBRUARY
18

Find out what the single most important thing is about your job, and then make sure it gets done every single day.

Even if nothing else gets done in a day, **make sure that one thing gets done.**

FEBRUARY
19

I just saw a television commercial for a popular pain reliever. The guy in the commercial is a mover who has problems with his knees. If you happen to see this commercial, you'll notice that the mover weighs about 300 pounds! No wonder his knees hurt; they are carrying around 150 pounds more than they were engineered to carry. This guy "fixes" his problem with a pain reliever. Actually, he is making his problem worse. **That pain is a *clue*!** The clue is to lose some weight! Instead, he is masking his problem so he won't notice it as he continues to get fatter and fatter. He is numbing himself to his real problem. Hey, Tubbo, you want your knees to hurt less? Listen to the pain and go after the *real* problem: your weight!

This approach is typical of what we do in all areas of life and business. We mask our problems so we won't notice them, hoping they will go away if we can't feel them.

This happens with our physical selves: Just numb yourself to the pain, and you won't have to deal with its real cause.

It also happens with our finances. People shop to feel better about the fact that they don't have any money; shopping numbs the pain. But shopping is causing the pain!

It happens in our jobs and in our relationships and in every other area of our lives too. We spend money and time and energy fixing the symptom instead of dealing with the real problem. The real problem can almost always be found looking back at you from your mirror. You are the problem. How you live, what you say or don't say, what you do or don't do, whom you hire and whom you don't fire, what you eat or don't eat, what you spend and how you spend it: These are your real problems.

Want a better life? Go after the cause of your problem. Don't mask the problem. Don't dull the pain. Instead, feel the pain and ask yourself what is really causing it. Then attack the cause!

FEBRUARY
20

When you **willingly share** part of what you have earned with others, it magically comes back to you. I don't know why it works, but I know it works.

FEBRUARY
21

Life is made up not of the haves and the have-nots, but of **the wills and the will-nots.**

FEBRUARY
22

Nobody ever wrote down a plan for being unsuccessful.

Unsuccessful is what happens when you don't have a plan.

FEBRUARY
23

We live in a black-and-white world. Stop
buying the idea about life not being black
or white. Things are either right or wrong,
good or bad, black or white. Stop rational-
izing your stupid behavior by putting it
in that gray area. When confronted with
a question they don't want to answer,
people always say, "That's a gray area."
There is no gray area.
Begin to think in absolutes, and you will
find that life is much easier. Making decisions is also much easier when you think
in terms of absolutes. Your excuses won't
hold water either, which will move you toward success much faster.

FEBRUARY
24

Don't expect respect
if you don't show respect.

FEBRUARY 25

If it is on your ass,
then it is not an asset.

That line is not original Larry, but it is one of my favorites. Get a grip on what is important, what matters, and what has value when it comes to your money. If it depreciates, then it is not an asset.

FEBRUARY
26

Do what you said you would do, when you said you would do it, the way you said you would do it.

That is all anyone wants from you. That is all that customers want from the people and the company they do business with. That is all that employees want from their employers. That is all that employers want from their employees. That is all that you want from your kids or your spouse or your significant other. And that is all they want from you.

FEBRUARY
27

Don't brag. It's obnoxious and it alienates others.

FEBRUARY
28

Don't complain and don't whine.

First of all, no one cares about your complaints because they have problems of their own.

Second, you look like a victim and you lose your power when you victimize yourself.

Third, nobody likes a whiner.

(If February 29 is your birthday, it sucks that you only get a real birthday every four years.)

MARCH
1

Don't tolerate abuse, disrespect, or a lack of ethics or integrity
from your employer. Life is short, and
there are other jobs.

$$$$$$$$$$$$$$

MARCH
2

Money is freedom—freedom to do what you want, when you want, the way you want, and with whom you want. That's it. But isn't that enough?

$$$$$$$$$$$$$$

MARCH
3

You will not change until you first
become uncomfortable
with where or who you are.

MARCH
4

Your life is exactly the way you want it to be. **If you wanted it to be different, it would be different.** It's that simple.

So instead of complaining about your life, do something about it.

MARCH
5

Serve your customer well, whether you call your customer a client, co-worker, patient, or boss. Your rewards in life are in direct proportion to the service you provide.

MARCH
6

Stress comes from knowing what is right and doing what is wrong.

MARCH
7

A deal is a deal.

If you don't like the deal you made, that's tough. You made that deal. I don't care if it costs you money, if it is embarrassing, if it is hard to live with, if it is humiliating, or if it is inconvenient. You made the deal. Period.

MARCH
8

Kids get better when parents get better. Wives get better when husbands get better. Husbands get better when wives get better. Sales get better when salespeople get better. Customer service gets better when the people who deliver the customer service get better.

This is exactly how every single thing in life and business works. **Everything in life gets better** when you get better, and nothing in life gets better until you get better. So if you want your life to get better, get better!

MARCH 9

Most people don't seem to be able to recognize the correlation between their behavior and their results. Instead, they call it bad luck or they want to lay blame on society. **We are all living the consequences of our choices.** They may be painful, but those consequences are our lessons. Learn these lessons, and you can have whatever you are willing to work for. Ignore these lessons, and you will be doomed to repeat them and suffer the consequences until you do learn them.

$$$$$$$$$$$$$

MARCH
10

You can't go out and make more money.
It's impossible. You aren't the mint. You
can't print it when you run short. You have
to go out there and earn more money.
**You have to work for
it.**

$$$$$$$$$$$$$

MARCH
11

There are only two things you will never be without. One is your **reputation** and the other is your **credit rating.** You can ruin both in an instant, and you can spend a lifetime trying to fix them.

MARCH
12

The Hole Principle:

When you find yourself in a hole—stop digging. But remember: The shovel is in your hands. No one else put you in the hole. You did it yourself. You dug your own financial hole. You dug the hole that is your marriage. Your hands held the shovel when you created the crater you call your career. Stop blaming other people for the hole you are in, and then stop digging. Now start filling in the hole until you find yourself back on level ground again.

MARCH
13

People get fired, demoted, passed over for promotions and raises, and denied privi-leges for one reason more than any other: They didn't have the results to deserve anything better.

MARCH
14

Work hard on your job and **harder on yourself.**

MARCH
15

Friendship among co-workers is a bonus. It is not required, nor should it be forced or expected.

MARCH
16

Remember that you work for someone. The person you work for has the right to say what you do, when you do it, and how you do it because that person is paying your salary. If you don't like that or aren't willing to accept that, then go find another job. Find a job working for someone who doesn't care what you do, when you do it, or how you do it. You know, someone like you.

MARCH
17

Don't spend a lot of time and energy trying to make sure that people like you. Instead, work hard on being the kind of person that others respect. **Respect will take you a lot further.**

MARCH
18

If it's broken, **fix it fast** before the problem grows and spreads.

MARCH
19

Most people are horrible listeners. For them, listening is that short period of time when they are waiting for the other person to shut up so they can talk again. Truly listening to another person is one of the highest forms of respect you can show them.

MARCH
20

Firing is not something you do **to** someone. Firing is something you do **for**
someone.

$$$$$$$$$$$$$$$$

MARCH
21

It is better to spend money on a **good attorney** than on a bad employee.

$$$$$$$$$$$$$$$$

MARCH
22

There are only two ways to lose weight. Eat less and exercise more. Don't complicate it. If you are fat, get off your big ol' butt and exercise, and try eating a little less along the way. **The results will amaze you.**

MARCH
23

Want to know how to stop smoking?

Stop putting cigarettes in your mouth.

MARCH
24

We all do what we do for one reason and one reason only, and that is to serve others well. Understand that **the better we serve others, the better we will in turn be served.**

MARCH
25

You can **never** build yourself up by tearing others down.

MARCH
26

Become the employee that your company can't live without.

Become the person that your customers can't live without.

Become the person that your company, your boss, your coworkers, and your customers count on, need, and want to have around.

That is job security at its best.

MARCH
27

Pretend I am your boss for a minute.

Here is my position: **Just do your damn job.** Don't complain about it. If you aren't willing to do that, then don't be surprised when I fire your lazy ass and tell you to get your butt out of my business. Remember, I'm the boss. I make the rules. I am held accountable for you. I am responsible for you. Your results are my results, and I am unwilling to take the blame for the fact that you won't do your job. Got it? Seems completely fair to me. If you have a problem with that, then I know exactly what kind of employee you are.

MARCH
28

Constructive criticism is a stupid concept. To construct means to build up. To criticize is to tear down. Pick one. You can't do both at the same time.

MARCH
29

Whining about your problem only prolongs the problem.

MARCH
30

I was raised to open doors for people. I open doors for women, for anyone whose arms are full, and for anyone who is older than I am. Almost no one says "Thank you." They walk past me like I'm the doorman. Of course I always say "You're welcome!" very politely as a reminder that I have been courteous to them and they owe me a thank-you for it.

Now, I want to make it clear that I don't hold doors open for others because I want to hear them say "Thank you." **I do it because it is what should be done.** I do it because I was raised to behave that way. I am not going to stop being courteous just because others aren't. I do it because I am hoping the world will wake up and be grateful when someone extends some common courtesy—which has become anything but common.

MARCH
31

Doing better is the result of deciding to do better and then taking action on that deci- sion. **Get busy!**

APRIL
1

The only things your kids know about money is what you have taught them. You set the example. Don't expect your kids to learn how to spend their money wisely if they have watched you squander yours on stupid stuff. **Your choices will become their choices.**

APRIL
2

Stop living backward and start living for-ward. **Begin with the end in mind.**

APRIL
3

The three main reasons people are not successful:

1. They are stupid.
2. They are lazy.
3. They don't give a damn.

APRIL
4

If you don't have much going wrong in your life, then you don't have much going on in your life.

APRIL
5

It's not how many hours you put into the
work, but **how much work
you put into the hours.**

APRIL
6

Be on time. There is never an excuse for being late.

APRIL
7

What you think about, talk about, and get off your ass and do something about **comes about.**

APRIL
8

"You can be whatever you want to be, do whatever you want to do, and have whatever you want to have."

That is a lie.

If you are short, fat, and ugly, that supermodel thing probably isn't going to work out for you.

You can do what you have the innate talent to do, depending on the time and effort you are willing to dedicate to developing your potential. You can always do more than you think you can, but you can't do just anything you want.

And you certainly can't have whatever you want. You can have the things you believe you deserve when you take action toward achieving them by utilizing your abilities, your thoughts, and your words.

APRIL
9

To make positive change in your life, you first have to get a little negative about your life.

APRIL
10

People are stupid.

Don't believe me? Consider this: People smoke knowing it will shorten their lives. People get drunk and drive their cars. People eat things they know aren't good for them. People fail to plan their futures, forget to schedule annual health checkups, expect schools to discipline their kids, spend all of their savings, and destroy the environment.

Like I said, people are stupid.

APRIL
11

Look at the numbers, look at the facts, listen to the experts, and then **trust your gut.**

APRIL
12

You can circle up, hug it out, hold hands, and sing "Kumbaya" for the rest of your life, but **until you accept responsibility** for your mistakes, then get over it and get busy fixing your life, you are going to be miserable.

APRIL
13

Find a religion that asks only that you
love your fellow man.
Find one that causes you to stop judging
others and teaches you to help others.
When you do, I bet it won't have the words
"First" or "Southern" in its name.

APRIL
14

Hang around smart people and it just might rub off on you. Hang around stupid people and I guarantee that it will rub off on you. **Stupidity is contagious!**

$$$$$$$$$$$$$$$$

APRIL
15

It is better to pay taxes on the money you
have than not to pay taxes on money you
don't have.

$$$$$$$$$$$$$$$

APRIL
16

A good divorce is better than a
bad marriage.

APRIL
17

You love people not because of who they **are but in spite of who they are.**

I have been married for more than twenty-five years, and this statement makes perfect sense to both my wife and me. I also raised two boys who are now grown men. Getting them to that point made me understand it even more.

APRIL
18

Kids are a major pain in the butt. They are dirty, messy, inconvenient, and expensive. Yet they are the coolest things that can happen to you. Take good care of them—you are going to need them when you get old!

APRIL
19

Want to teach your kids about sex? Trust
me, they will learn about the mechanics
long before you get around to talking
to them about it. These are the things
you should focus on: **respect;
responsibility; safety.**
They can figure out the rest without you.
These three things they need your help
with.

APRIL
20

A guaranteed way to avoid criticism:

Say nothing. Do nothing. Be nothing.

APRIL
21

You can't get a good deal from **a bad guy.**

APRIL 22

If **the most important thing** gets done, regardless of what it is, nothing else really matters much.

APRIL
23

Guilt serves no purpose. The past is just that: passed! Gone. Slipped away. Not to be repeated. If you need to make restitution, then do it. If you messed up, apologize. If you are forgiven for your mistake, give thanks and move on. If you are not forgiven, move on anyway. Forgive yourself, learn from the experience, and act differently next time. At that point, it's over. **Don't bother with guilt.**

APRIL
24

"It is what it is." People say that when they want an excuse for the way things are. **That is a total load of crap.** How about saying something much more accurate, like "It is the way I allow it to be." Or how about "It is the way it is because that's what I'm willing to accept." Or "It is what it is because that's all I expect." Or "It is what it is because I'm too damn stupid and lazy to make it any different than it is." I have never bought into the whole "It is what it is" mentality. Instead, my life has always been based on "It is the way I make it!" Same with "Que Sera, Sera," that idiotic song so popular when I was growing up that said, "Whatever will be, will be / The future's not ours to see / Que sera, sera." The future *is* yours to see. The future is also yours to create. You just have to be willing to do it.

APRIL
25

When people say **"Let me be honest with you,"** it means that in the past, they haven't been.

APRIL
26

Never say anything stupid like "It can't get any worse than this!" That is a challenge you do not want to issue. If there is one thing I have learned, **it can always get worse!**

APRIL
27

The less people have to say, the more they
feel compelled to say it.

APRIL
28

Have you heard the motivational idiots say, "You can do the impossible"? No, you can't. The very definition of the word "impossible" means that it can't be done! If it can be done, then it wasn't impossible at all. It was hard to do, perhaps, but it wasn't impossible.

APRIL
29

**Implement now—
perfect later.**

APRIL
30

You don't have to be good to start.
**But you do have to
start to be good.**

MAY
1

Human beings are the only species on earth that knowingly chooses to be less than it has the potential to be. No other living thing in nature chooses to be less than it could be. Only people do that. Did you ever see a tree grow to about six feet tall and say, "Eh, I'm good right here," and then stop growing? No, a tree grows to be as tall as it can be. A tree grows as many leaves as it can. A tree puts down as many roots as it can. A tree bears as much fruit as it possibly can. Trees continue to grow and produce as long as they are alive.

All plants grow to be as big as they can be. The same applies to every living thing on earth—except people. Rats, horses, pigs, and dogs all grow as much as they can. Fish and worms and amoebas all do the same. Every living species grows, develops, and produces as much as it possibly can—everything except people. People are the only beings in the universe that choose to be less than they can be. They get to a point in their lives and just stop. They choose to quit learning, quit growing, and quit developing. They choose to quit earning and quit producing and quit contributing. People stop growing because they choose to, not because they have to or need to or should.

MAY
2

It is better to **underpromise and overperform** than it is to overpromise and underperform.

MAY
3

Stop focusing on what you don't want to happen. What a complete waste of time and energy that is! Instead, **focus on the results you would like** to have happen in every area of your life; then go to work to make those things happen.

$$$$$$$$$$$$$$

MAY
4

Money comes to you just as it goes from you.

If you let it go begrudgingly, it will come to you in the same way.

$$$$$$$$$$$$$$

MAY
5

It doesn't matter where you start out in
life; **it only matters where
you end up.**

MAY
6

Have good, healthy arguments. Arguments are good things. When two people always agree, one of them is no longer necessary.

MAY
7

When your kids' rooms are a mess, shut the door. Save yourself the frustration of telling them one more time to clean up their rooms. When it is important enough for them to do it, they will. In the meantime, **shut the door.**

MAY
8

Hang in there. **Don't give up.** But don't be an idiot about it either. Eventually there comes a time to walk away and let it go. As the saying goes, "When you find yourself on a dead horse, get off."

$$$$$$$$$$$$$$$

MAY

9

"Stuff costs too much!"

No, it doesn't. The fact is that you just don't have enough money. **Don't blame the stuff for costing too much.** Stuff just costs what it costs. It's your fault if you don't have enough money.

$$$$$$$$$$$$$$$

MAY
10

When someone says to you, **"I want to tell you this for your own good,"** you need to know that it is not for your own good. It is for their own good. Don't be victimized by their controlling behavior.

MAY
11

Is the glass half full or half empty?

Who cares?

The real question is this: Does whatever is in the glass quench your thirst? In other words, does your attitude work for you? Sometimes the old positive attitude is a good thing and sometimes you have to get negative in order for change to take place. **Use what works.**

MAY
12

I use a lot of four-letter words. Here is the one that works best in almost any situation: **"next."** When someone ticks me off, I just try to say **"next."** When something bad happens and doesn't go my way, I just try to say **"next."** I'm not as good at it as I would like to be, but it beats most of the other four-letter words I use, which don't do me any good at all.

MAY
13

I got the best marriage advice I ever heard from a couple that had been married for sixty-seven years. This is what they told me: **"Just let the other person be who they are and put up with it."**

MAY
14

Success comes from what you **do,** not from what you **say** you are going to do.

MAY
15

Bad things happen to everyone. You don't have the market cornered on bad luck. Besides, it is not what happens to you that matters. It's what you do about what happens to you that matters.

MAY
16

Your income is going to be on average that of your five closest friends'.

Don't have enough money? **Get some richer friends.**

No kidding. Dump them and get some friends with some money.

MAY
17

It's rarely personal.

MAY
18

What do you want out of life? Is it written down? Do you have a plan? Are you learning what it takes to make it happen? Do you do something every day to bring you closer to it? Or do you only want it? If want is all you have, more want is all you are ever going to get. **You have to go past just wanting and put together a plan** to make sure you get it.

MAY
19

My roof—my rules. Somewhere along the line, that parenting message has become passé. It shouldn't have. If I feed and clothe my kids, and they live in my house and are underage, then they must live by the rules I establish. Those rules exist to protect my children. I created those rules out of love for my children.

When they are of legal age and can feed and clothe themselves and provide their own shelter out of their own earnings, then they can establish their own rules.

What's wrong with that as a parenting rule? It's fair. It makes perfect sense, and it is grounded in love and caring.

MAY
20

In business, **good results cover up a multitude of sins.**

MAY
21

If you have to ask whether it is right or wrong, it's wrong. Just having to ask the question gives you the answer. If it is the right thing to do, you know it without ever having to question it. **Just trust your gut.**

MAY
22

Having a bad day at work today? How sad. Why should the company suffer because you aren't happy today? Why should anyone care that you are having a bad day? Customers still need to be served. Boxes still need to be shipped. The copier still needs to be fixed. Telephones still need to be answered. If you are paid to do those things, then **you must get them done** whether or not you are having a bad day.

MAY
23

Business is never really bad. People are just bad at being in business.

MAY
24

Success is never easy.

If it were, there would be many more successful people in the world. Success comes from hard work, staying focused, striving for excellence, consistently delivering excellence, discipline, and much, much more. These concepts are not complicated; they are simple ideas that require hard work.

MAY
25

Get this straight: **There is simply no excuse for not doing well.**

MAY
26

If you make a promise, keep it. If you give your word, don't go back on it. If you say you are going to be there, be there—and be there when you said you would be there. **If you mess up, admit it and accept the consequences.** If someone gives you money for a product or service you provide, be at least a little grateful and friendly to that person.

MAY
27

We work together.
   We are not family.
   We are not related.
   I don't have to like you. I don't have to spend time with you. **I just have to work with you.**
   That's all I have to do with you—everything else is a matter of choice.

MAY
28

Ladies, **men are idiots when it comes to dealing with women.** You confuse us, confound us, and intimidate us. Our mouths and brains don't work in sync when we are around you. We say stuff that to us sounds perfectly innocent and complimentary. Please, if you don't like it, let us know. Set us straight. We will probably be astounded, as we are all so ignorant about these matters. So tell us, wait for our humble apology, and forgive us. Please.

MAY
29

A disorganized workspace means disorganized work habits. A sloppy work environment equals sloppy results. Don't say "That's how I work best!" No one works better surrounded by chaos. **Clean up** and get organized so you can focus.

MAY
30

T-N-T.

Today, not tomorrow. This should be the motto of every employee, every manager, every leader, and every business. If it's a good idea, do it today, not tomorrow. Good ideas rarely get better over time.

MAY
31

There is always enough time to do what is important to you. If you aren't doing the right thing in your life, it's because it isn't important enough to you to do it. You can fill in the blank on this one. Reading isn't important to you. Personal development isn't important to you. Saving isn't important to you. Exercise isn't important to you. Just know that if you aren't doing it, whatever it is, it's because it isn't important to you.

JUNE
1

Practice does not make perfect.

"Practice makes perfect" is a stupid thing to say. If you practice the wrong thing, you don't get better; you just learn how to do the wrong thing extremely well.

Practice makes permanent, not perfect.

JUNE
2

Did you ever hear someone say, "Well, you never know . . ." How can you never know? Don't you know at least some of the time?

JUNE
3

Talk, talk, talk. I get so tired of it. I agree with the Elvis song that says, "A little less conversation, a little more action please." Don't tell me what you plan to do, want to do, think you should do, or are going to do.

Just show me what you are doing. **Actions change things.** Words don't.

JUNE
4

There are no secrets.

There is no new information. The things it takes to be successful today are the same things it has taken to be successful throughout history: accountability, honesty, integrity, ethical behavior, fairness, work, charity, service. These are the things that never change; they are the foundation of all success.

JUNE
5

Stop periodically throughout the day and ask yourself: Does this really matter? Is what I'm doing contributing to my own overall well-being or to the well-being of the company I'm working for? Am I really getting something done, or am I just killing time? Is this the most important use of my time right now?

JUNE
6

Never get bogged down with the should-get-dones or the wouldn't-it-be-nice-to-get-dones or the easy-to-dos. Focus on the must-get-dones—and make sure they get done!

JUNE
7

Take your **job** seriously, not yourself.

JUNE
8

If you don't have five great books on your desk, then you aren't keeping up. If you don't have a couple of business books, a novel, a biography, and something light for pure entertainment as well as a stack of magazines, then you aren't gaining momentum. Plus, you will be a boring conversationalist. **Read!**

JUNE
9

The next time you hear yourself saying "I don't like my job," remember this: No one cares. **You aren't paid to like your job.** You are paid to *do* your job.

JUNE
10

Excellence does not come from passion, enjoyment, love, or fun. It comes from experience. It comes from screwing up and doing it wrong until you finally, finally, finally get it right. And it comes from good old-fashioned hard work. The other things help, but alone they are mostly hot air. Sweat changes things—not hot air.

JUNE
11

Be honest.

Every time and without exception, even when it's hard.

In fact, especially when it's hard.

JUNE
12

If you can't figure out how to get your job done in the number of hours you are paid to work, it probably means you are goofing off when you are supposed to be working.

JUNE
13

Never tolerate poor performance in yourself or others.

JUNE
14

Don't measure busywork. Don't measure activity. **Measure accomplishment.** What people do doesn't matter as much as what they get done.

$$$$$$$$$$$$$$

JUNE
15

Never let your mouth write a check that
your ass can't cash.

$$$$$$$$$$$$$$

JUNE
16

**Never tolerate
mediocrity.**

JUNE
17

Anytime you don't give your best effort, you are **stealing.**

You are stealing from your company because they hired you and they pay your salary for your best effort. You are stealing from your coworkers because they have to pick up your slack. You are stealing from your customers because they are paying retail to receive your best effort. Most of all, you are stealing from yourself because you have robbed yourself of the satisfaction that comes from doing your best.

JUNE
18

All talk is just that: talk. All the words written on these pages are just that: words. If you want things to get better, take action. Don't just talk about it. Don't just read and think about it. **Do it.**

JUNE
19

Don't like bad service? What are you doing about it? Do you speak up? Do you complain? Do you ask for a manager? Do you tell others about your experience? Do you contact the Better Business Bureau? Do you write letters? Post a blog? Write an e-mail? Or do you just take it, mumble to yourself, and decide not to go back there? Until you refuse to accept bad service and speak up against bad service, you are doomed to receive bad service.

JUNE
20

There are people who are going to die from "terminal professionalism."

Lighten up!

Are you suffering from "terminal professionalism"? Take a break. Don't take things so seriously when you are not at work.

JUNE
21

"As long as you feel good about yourself, you can do anything!"

That's a total lie.

You never made one positive change in your whole life when you felt good about yourself. You make positive change in your life when you **get uncomfortable** with yourself.

JUNE
22

When you read a book, **read for intent rather than for content.** Books have a lot of information—sometimes too much. So don't try to absorb all of it. Look for the central theme, the overriding concept, and the one great idea that the author is trying to convey. When you get to the end of the book, write the one great idea in the back of the book so that in a few years you can return to the book and review what you learned.

JUNE
23

Why you want to accomplish something is more important than how you are going to accomplish something. There are as many ways to do something as there are people who have done it. Besides, spending too much time worrying about how can bog you down. **Focus on the why.** With a strong enough why, you can endure any how.

$$$$$$$$$$$$$$$

JUNE
24

The ideal plan for your money:

Save 10 percent.
Invest 10 percent.
Give away 10 percent.
Live on the remaining 70 percent.

$$$$$$$$$$$$$$$

JUNE
25

Some people have all the luck. You've heard that line. You have probably even said it. Maybe you have said this: "With my luck . . ." And then you follow it with some horrible thing that you don't want to have happen.

Forget luck. Luck is where opportunity meets preparation. Are you prepared to take advantage of opportunities as they come your way? No? Then don't expect any luck. Once you are prepared for all the opportunities that come along, you will have lots of luck. Go get prepared and learn to recognize and take advantage of your opportunities.

JUNE
26

When you work, work!
When you play, play!
Don't mix the two.

JUNE
27

I think it is sad when I see mothers and fathers trying to be their kids' best friends. Kids don't want you to be their buddy; they want you to be their parent. You can't be one of the gang and maintain the respect that is required for you to be a good parent. My boys and I are friends—good friends. We talk openly about everything going on in their lives. Yet there is a line between friend and parent that we don't cross.

JUNE
28

People often ask me what books they should read.

Here is a clue: Don't read what poor people read. **Read what rich people read.**

JUNE
29

Everyone screws up. We all make mistakes. We are human; it's what we do. If you are living without making any mistakes, know one thing: You are dead. Here is the key: **Learn from your mistakes.** It's okay to make lots of mistakes, but it's not okay to make the same mistake over and over again. At some point, you need to get a clue.

JUNE
30

The first step you have to take in changing your life is to **make the decision to change your life.** All things that happen begin with a decision. If you decide that you really want to do better, you will take the necessary steps to do what it takes to do better. Most people never do as well as they expect or desire because they haven't made that first decision.

JULY
1

Ethics is a matter of black and white—not gray. It's either right or wrong, good or bad, hello or good-bye. You are either in the way or on the way.

Easy to say but hard to figure out? Not really. How do you know whether something is the right thing to do or the wrong thing to do? If you have to ask, it's the wrong thing. And there you have your answer. So do the right thing even when it is unpopular or might cost you money or be embarrassing. In the long run, consistently doing the right thing will pay off every time, without exception. Do the right thing when it comes to your kids, your spouse, your family, your boss, your employees, your customers, and the stranger in the car next to you or the one you pass on the street, and do the right thing with your taxes too! Never compromise your future success or shortchange your present success by doing less than the right thing in every circumstance.

JULY
2

I believe in selfishness.

The best way for me to serve others is to selfishly serve myself well. When I take the time to feel good physically, I do a better job. That requires some selfishness. When I do what I want to do, I am better at it, and the better I am at what I do, the better others are served by what I do.

It is possible to give so much of yourself away that you compromise the quality of what you have to give.

JULY
3

We don't have a customer service problem as much as **we have a parent-ing problem.**

The reason the kid who hands you your cup of coffee can't look you in eye, acknowledge your presence, greet you, or say thank you is because he wasn't raised to do any of those things.

That's a parenting issue.

JULY
4

In America we talk a good game when it comes to patriotism.

We salute the flag, brag that America is the greatest country on earth—we talk a good game when it comes to patriotism. But unless you practice democracy by voting, you don't deserve to enjoy it. You also don't get the right to gripe about it.

I don't care how you vote. I really don't. I would love for elections to go my way, but if they don't, I will live with the results. My point is simple: **Vote.** Vote for anyone you want to and for any reason you have. But do it.

JULY
5

The problem with most self-help is that it's way too much **help** and not nearly enough **self.**

What self-help should really be telling you is that you made your mess and it's up to you to clean it up.

Don't always be looking for help outside yourself. The best helping hand you will ever find is attached to your own wrist.

JULY
6

Most people live in the middle, leading mediocre lives, thinking mediocre thoughts, doing mediocre things, and achieving mediocre results. Their incomes fall in the median range. Their houses are in the median range. Their entire lives are median, mediocre, and stuck deeply in the middle. Sadly, most people don't even recognize their predicament because everyone they know is stuck there in the middle with them. Get out of the middle. It's boring. Move to the edge. **The edge is where the fun is,** where the money is, and where true self-satisfaction is. The best part of living on the edge is that it isn't crowded at all.

JULY
7

When it comes to results, people don't ask how; they ask how many.

Quantifiable results interest people much more than the method used to obtain those results. As long as your methods are legal, ethical, moral, and reasonable, that's all anyone should care about.

JULY
8

Some people go to overweight doctors who smoke to find out how to be healthy. **Does that make sense?** You are an idiot if you go to a doctor who is choosing to destroy his or her own health. "Fat doctor" equals "lousy doctor" in my mind. A doctor who smokes cigarettes should be stripped of his medical license. Licensing a doctor who violates such a basic tenet of being healthy makes as much sense as passing out day-care certifications to convicted sex offenders. Avoid doctors who are fat, who smoke, who automatically think that drugs and surgery are the first answer to everything that ails you, and who make you wait more than thirty minutes to see them.

JULY
9

People say they want great kids. Of course they say that; who doesn't want to raise good kids?

But the reality is that the average amount of time parents spend a week in meaningful conversation with their children is three and a half minutes. Two hundred and ten seconds per week. Thirty seconds per day.

Sure, we want good kids, just not enough to talk to them. This should make you mad or ill or both.

JULY
10

There is **never** a need to have more than three credit cards.

You don't need to open a store credit card to save 10 percent on today's purchase. That's a great trick that makes you think you are saving 10 percent, but the reality is that you now have one more credit card at a high interest rate that will reflect negatively on your credit rating.

Forget the 10 percent savings and realize that you don't need another credit card. Besides, when you buy something at 40 percent off, you aren't saving 40 percent. You are spending 60 percent. If you weren't planning on buying it at full price, you aren't saving anything.

JULY
11

Businesses exist for one reason and only one reason: to make a profit. The most profitable companies serve their customers well. They ensure their profitability by employing people who are worth more than they cost.

If your business isn't doing well, it's because you aren't serving your customers well or employing the right kind of people.

JULY
12

People drink and drive, get in accidents, and then want to sue bars and bartenders for overserving them.

People spill hot coffee in their laps and sue the people who made the coffee too hot. Yet if the coffee wasn't hot, they would complain about that too.

Stop suing people because you are clumsy or because you don't know when you've had enough!

JULY
13

People will ask for advice—even beg for advice. It seems they will do anything for advice. They will even pay for advice. Then they won't take the advice.

People will go to a rich guy for advice on what it takes to be rich. The rich guy tells them exactly what to do. Do they do it? No. In fact, sometimes they even argue about the advice.

Your doctor will tell you exactly what to do to be healthier. Will you do it? Probably not. You obviously know better than any stupid doctor who's received medical training for seven-plus years.

Why bother asking for advice if the only opinion you respect enough to consider is your own?

JULY
14

After all is said and done, **more is said than done.**

JULY
15

You don't want any of the things you say you want. Those are just words. **You want what you have.** That's why you have it. If you wanted something different, you would have something different. Or you would at least be taking action to get something different from what you have.

It's time you took a good hard look at the truth. Stop lying to yourself. The truth is that your life is the way you want it to be.

JULY
16

People treat you **the way you teach them to treat you.**

JULY
17

Success is a process of elimination.

You must eliminate the nonsuccessful behavior in your life in order to make room for the successful behavior.

JULY
18

There comes a point when you should have figured out on your own what it takes to do okay. **Pay attention.** Look around, watch what other people are doing, and get a clue as to what works and what doesn't work. Then stop doing all the stupid things that don't work.

JULY
19

I contend that every person knows exactly what he or she should be doing in every situation for things to be better. They may not know all they need to do, but they know something they could do. The really stupid part is that while people always know something they could do, they rarely do it. That's the part that ticks me off the most. You know what to do and yet you aren't doing it? **What kind of person are you?**

$$$$$$$$$$$$$$$

JULY
20

Hope is not a wealth strategy. Wishful thinking is not a plan for success.

$$$$$$$$$$$$$$$

JULY
21

Many people believe that their results are just their lot in life. They think, "These are the cards I have been dealt and I have to play them."

No, you don't have to play them. The nice thing about life is that you can always refuse to play the hand you have been dealt; you can ask for a redeal. The good news is, you are the dealer. **You can deal yourself a new hand.**

JULY
22

There is no such thing as being fashion-ably late. **Late is rude.** Late is disrespectful. Rude and disrespectful are never fashionable.

JULY
23

If you want to build a house, **you begin with the end in mind.** You visualize the finished product and then create the plans to make your vision come to fruition. You hire an architect, find a builder, and go to work. Your general contractor keeps a close watch on all the subcontractors to make sure they are doing their jobs and that the project stays on track. You put your time and your energy and your money into the project to make sure that what you picture in your mind is what you actually end up with.

This is exactly what parenting is about too. You begin with the end in mind. Only in parenting, you are the architect, the builder, and the general contractor. There are some subcontractors in there too. Those subcontractors include grandparents, family, friends, babysitters, teachers, coaches, and others who will have periodic and temporary responsibility for your child's development. As the general contractor you are in charge of those subcontractors to make sure they do their job and help you keep the overall project on track.

JULY
24

Remember the old joke "Why does a dog lick himself?" Answer: "Because he can." Why do people do what they do? Because they can.

For the most part, people will get away with whatever they can if there are no consequences. **Consequences control behavior.** I am a big believer in enforcing consequences and allowing people to learn from the pain of their bad decisions.

JULY
25

To have what you have never had and to get something you have never gotten, **you have to do something you have never done.**

JULY
26

Many of us have reached a point where we don't expect much from other people. We have become so jaded by bad experiences that we don't expect people to be anything but stupid.

Yet this kind of thinking is a mistake. I have discovered that people will either live up to or live down to whatever expectations we set for them. **Expect the best from others and you increase your chances of getting it.**

While you do that, expect more from yourself too. You might be disappointed when people don't deliver, but it is better to be disappointed by expecting a lot and getting nothing than by expecting nothing and getting it.

JULY
27

One of the reasons people aren't successful is that they can't create a picture of
what success should look like in their
lives. They can see success happening in
other people's lives, but they can't see success happening in their own lives.
**They are stuck in a
rut,** seeing their life the way it is or the
way it has been instead of the way it could
be. You have to move beyond that vision of
the way your life has always looked and
begin to picture your life as you want it to
look.

JULY
28

Funny how you don't think eating healthy foods and exercising are important at all until you have a heart attack. Then your health becomes your biggest priority. Why did you have to have the heart attack for it to become important? **Wouldn't it have been cheaper and less painful not to have the heart attack?**

JULY
29

Your time, energy, and money always go to what is important to you.

If you aren't putting your time, energy, and money into something, then it shows **you don't give a damn about it.**

JULY
30

What could possibly be more important to you than living up to your full potential? To live as prosperously as you can? To be as healthy as you can? To enjoy your friends and family? To be a good parent? To be a good spouse?

Nothing is more important than living up to your full potential. Period.

JULY
31

Speakers and authors will tell you that success is hard. And that is exactly what you want it to be. You want it to be hard because when you buy into the mistaken idea that success is hard, you have an excuse for not being successful. After all, it's hard!

Don't buy it. **Success is simple.** It comes down to a handful of good ideas like taking responsibility, living with integrity, being honest, and working hard. Does it take more than that? Of course it does. However, if you can master those simple ideas first, and then do a little study, you will discover what else it takes. And you will find out that everything is simple.

AUGUST
1

The Beatles were right. **All you need is love.** Of course, good health and a little money also help.

AUGUST
2

Every good thing that has happened in my life has been the result of my decision to make it happen. The same applies to you and your life. **Your decisions will shape your future.** You must decide that you are willing to do whatever it takes to live the life you want and the life you deserve.

AUGUST
3

Kids must learn to accept and handle the discipline they receive at home. If your kids aren't able to deal with discipline at home, how will they handle discipline at school? Or as adults in their work environment? Answer: They won't.

Ill-behaved children who abuse or disrespect the authority of their parents will disrespect the authority of their teachers and their bosses. If you don't impose and enforce compliance with your rules as a parent, you are **dooming the future of your child** at school and ruining their chances to be productive in their jobs.

AUGUST
4

Be generous—not only with your money, but also with your time. Give to people who need what you have more than you do. And never think you have too little to give some of what you have to others. You always have enough to share.

AUGUST
5

Discipline is a code of conduct by which you live your life and raise your kids. Punishment is what happens when you break the code.

AUGUST
6

Carve out some time each day for education.

Don't say things like "I don't have time to read." That's just plain stupid, and it's offensive to those of us who make the time to read. You have plenty of time to read.

If it is important enough to you, then you will find the time to do it. That principle works across the board. You will find the time for whatever is important to you. Begin with fifteen minutes. Everyone can find fifteen minutes a day to read. Start with fifteen minutes and build from there.

AUGUST
7

People spend all week planning for their day off, but they don't spend one minute planning the rest of their lives. When it comes to that day off, they decide exactly what they are going to do, who they are going to do it with, how long it is going to take, and what it will cost them.

Why not do the same things for your life? Figure out what work you are going to do, what kind of fun you are going to have, who you are going to do it with, and how much it is going to cost.

AUGUST
8

Don't think you can make someone into the person you want them to be. **People change—but not often.** It is damn near impossible to change someone, and the challenge is rarely worth the effort. Save time: Find the right person from the get-go.

AUGUST
9

Don't cut your kids too much slack. You do your children a great disservice by being too lenient.

AUGUST
10

Become HWP. Don't know what that is? Good. That means you aren't cruising the Internet dating sites or reading the personal ads in the local paper. It means "height-weight proportionate." Get that way.

AUGUST
11

If things start to become complicated, stop, regroup, and start over.

Success is always simple. **Not easy, but simple.**

AUGUST
12

Be willing to be the fool sometimes. The ability to make fun of yourself is critical to having fun.

Take your job seriously, take your health seriously, take your finances and your family seriously, but don't take yourself too seriously.

AUGUST
13

Own a whoopee cushion and red socks. A crowded elevator and a whoopee cushion are a guaranteed recipe for laughter. This works better for guys. We think farts are the funniest things on the planet.

Regarding the red socks: Buy a pair and wear them just one time, and I promise you won't take yourself so seriously after that. For years I have said that the epitaph on my tombstone should be "He was a red-sock guy in a brown-sock world."

AUGUST
14

The key to any good relationship is the willingness to go more than halfway. This works with your kids, your spouse, your coworkers, and your customers. That old saying "I'll meet you halfway" may work in a deal negotiation, but it won't work in a personal relationship. You have to go way beyond halfway to keep a relationship working. You even have to go more than all the way. You have to go as far as it takes to get along, and then you have to go a little farther.

$$$$$$$$$$$$$$$$

AUGUST
15

Money is the result of serving people well. Serving people is an honorable thing, and it's hard work. Money is the result of hard work.

Having money in your life is a wonderful thing. It pays for college for your kids. It pays for health care when you and the people you love get sick. It takes care of your mom and dad when they get old and need help. It feeds the homeless and helps those who are less fortunate. It pays your taxes to build roads and provide fire and police protection. It is to be appreciated, saved, invested, and enjoyed.

$$$$$$$$$$$$$$$

AUGUST
16

There are financial gurus out there trying to teach people the secret to getting rich. But the truth is there are as many ways to get rich as there are rich people. There is no single way to get rich.

Regardless of which way you choose, you aren't going to get rich until you stop doing the things that are keeping you broke. I don't teach people to get rich; I teach them what it takes to stop being broke. If you teach someone how to get rich before you teach him how to stop being broke, he will only go broke again in a bigger way. He may get rich, but he will still have the habits of a broke person. You have to teach someone how to stop living like a broke person and how to start living like a rich person before the money actually shows up.

AUGUST
17

Have lots of sex. When sex stops, the intimacy usually stops and the relationship deteriorates.

A note to all women: Men are pigs. Have sex with us and we will do whatever you want. We will talk; we will listen; we will carry out the trash. Don't have sex with us and we will still figure out a way to have it—it just won't be with you. That's the law of the jungle. Men want a sandwich and sex. We are uncomplicated that way. Use that information to your advantage.

AUGUST
18

Become stingy with your time. This means you have to get really good at saying no. When someone asks you to do something that doesn't fit your plan, say no. When someone wants you to spend your time doing something you don't want to do, say no. It's a simple process but sometimes hard to pull off.

AUGUST
19

Activity brings about more activity. Sitting on your ass just brings about more sitting on your ass.

AUGUST
20

Make a "thankful for" list.
List things like your house, your car, your friends, your abilities, your stuff, your family, and your job. Also list the things you wouldn't normally think of, like your health, what you know, and what you are learning.

As Zig Ziglar says, "The more you are thankful for what you have, the more you will have to be thankful for."

$$$$$$$$$$$$$$$

AUGUST
21

When asked to give to a charity, find out what percentage of the money actually goes to the cause and not to the administration of the cause. If the person asking you doesn't know the answer to that question, walk away or hang up. If more money goes to running the organization than goes to the cause itself, this is not a charity you want to be involved in.

$$$$$$$$$$$$$$$

AUGUST
22

Don't deny that a problem is a problem. People who say, "I don't have problems; I only have opportunities" are idiots. Some problems are not opportunities—they are problems. Recognize them as problems and deal with them appropriately. Denial is stupid, and it doesn't do anything but prolong the pain of the problem.

AUGUST
23

If you don't have any-thing of relevance to say, then please be quiet. Don't just prattle on just because you like to hear yourself talk. I know professional speakers like this. They are so in love with the sound of their own voice that the audience has quit listening long before they have finished talking.

AUGUST
24

Beware of the telephone. Don't let it interrupt what must be done. It's actually okay to let it ring and go to voice mail as long as you return your calls promptly. If you are on a phone call that is running long, the best way to get off the phone is to say, "I know you are busy and I need to let you go." No one will admit they aren't busy. Say that, and they will let you off the hook.

AUGUST
25

Begin each day by running through a little mental **"I am thankful"** exercise.

Open your eyes in the morning and be thankful you lived through the night—many didn't.

Be glad you have something to do that day and people to do it with.

Wait—you don't have anything to do or people to do it with? Then go find something to do and some people to do it with, and be thankful you found them.

AUGUST
26

A reporter asked me recently in an interview, "At the end of the day, what really matters?" My answer: "Not much."

Really, not much matters. At the end of the day, if you smiled more than you frowned, laughed more than you cried, told your family and friends that you love them, and had a pretty good time doing what you do for a living, then it was a good day.

Go to bed and say thanks.

AUGUST
27

Be authentic. Don't try to be someone you aren't. You will hate yourself for it, and the effort to maintain the façade will exhaust you. Be real.

Many won't like the real you, but that is better than having people adore the person that isn't you at all.

AUGUST
28

Don't worry about how many friends you have. It is better to have a few really good friends you can count on than a bunch of fair-weather friends who won't be there when you need them.

When it comes to friends, go for quality instead of quantity.

AUGUST
29

Be a good listener. The best friend you will ever have is one who will just listen. By the way, the emphasis is on the word "just." This is why my bulldog, Ralph, is my best friend. No judgment, only a calm acceptance of what I am saying. He doesn't understand a word I'm saying, but he loves me enough to listen. Be like Ralph.

AUGUST
30

Please don't buy into the idea that success is hard to achieve.

Those who tell you that success is hard are trying to undermine your success by playing to your weaker side. They are treating you like a sucker. Don't be a sucker for them. **Shun the idea that success is hard. It isn't.** The people who believe that success is hard want it to be hard. They want success to be hard so they will have a reason not to be successful. It's their primary excuse.

If you are one of those people who believes success is hard, then that's why you haven't been successful so far.

AUGUST
31

To be a good parent and role model for your child, you have to get beyond your own upbringing. You have to get past your own fears and prejudices so that you won't pass them on to your children. They will develop their own fears and prejudices without any help from you.

Free your kids from your past.

SEPTEMBER
1

The truth hurts; that's how you know it's the truth.

If someone comes up to you and says something really nice, they're probably lying to you!

SEPTEMBER 2

Telling people that passion is the key to success does those folks a great disservice. Somewhere down the road, they will discover that no one cares about or shares their passion. They will find out that while they are passionate, they haven't done the work to be really good, and they know nothing about selling, marketing, leadership, management, finance, their competition, serving customers, or all the other facets of a successful life or business. They are passionate, but they are passionately incompetent. They don't have the skills to excel. All they have is their passion.

Try cashing that at the bank.

SEPTEMBER
3

Motivational gurus have made trillions of dollars telling us that having a positive attitude is the key to success. Wrong! You can be positive all you want and still be positively wrong, positively lazy, and positively stupid.

I don't always have a great attitude. In fact, many times I have a really crappy attitude. That makes me a real human being. Things go wrong and affect my attitude. Luckily, I am not paid to be positive. You aren't paid for your great attitude either. **You are paid to do your job.** I'll take Mr. Crappy Attitude, who gets the work done, and you can have Mr. Positivity, who believes that there are no problems, only opportunities. I'll go with the guy who knows a problem when he sees it, gets ticked off by it, and solves it!

SEPTEMBER
4

Stand for something.

Draw more lines in the sand.

Be uncompromising in your expectations, your standards, and your values.

SEPTEMBER
5

Work when other people are not around: during lunch hours, before others come in, and after they go home. **People are a distraction**—avoid them when you have something important to get done.

SEPTEMBER
6

Want to get more done around the house?
Stand up.

You get very little done when sitting on your butt. This is a simple suggestion, and you are probably laughing at it right now, but you need to trust me on this one. Stand up and walk around your house. You will see a magazine that needs to be picked up or a pillow that needs to be straightened or a table that needs to be dusted or clothes that need to be washed or folded. You wouldn't see those things sitting on your butt in front of the television. Stand up and move around.

SEPTEMBER
7

Don't travel with a pillow. People who carry their own personal pillow on trips are idiots. Like there aren't any pillows where these people are going? I have traveled 250 days per year for nearly twenty years. I have stayed in hotels in cities all over the world, and so far, every single place I have traveled has had pillows. "But I can't sleep without my own pillow!" Grow up, you big baby; you aren't two years old! Leave your raggedy old pillow with the faded Strawberry Shortcake pillowcase on your bed and travel like a grown-up.

SEPTEMBER
8

Smart people rarely hang around stupid people unless they are related to them.

This also applies to how healthy you are and how happy you are. Fat people normally hang around other fat people. Happy people hang around other happy people—that is why they are happy; it's hard to be happy when you hang around whiny, sad, angry people! Get the picture?

Are you hanging around the kind of people you want to be like? If not, dump them and find new people to hang around. By the way, if your friends start dumping you, it's probably because they read this and don't want you as a friend any longer.

SEPTEMBER
9

Be confident.

There is no one who is not attracted to confidence. Women dig it. Men love it.

Confidence adds hair, drops ten pounds, and takes off ten years.

SEPTEMBER 10

Fat mommies and daddies have fat kids. People who don't read have kids who don't read. Parents who spend more than they earn raise kids who spend more than they earn. Kids who come from a household where the parents work hard and pay their bills on time usually end up doing the same. Children who watched their parents read books and enjoy them usually end up readers.

Your kids are a reflection of you. What image are you providing them to reflect?

SEPTEMBER
11

Don't expect perfection from your kids, especially when it comes to grades. Ask them to do their best, regardless of what that might be, and then be satisfied with that. Teach your kids to be satisfied with their best as well. **Being the best isn't important, but doing your best is.**

SEPTEMBER 12

What is the worst that could happen?

This is the question I always ask myself when I am afraid to do something. If the worst that can happen is "I'm going to die," then I don't do it. But that is rarely a possible result of anything I am going to attempt. Usually the worst that can happen is that I won't do as well as I had hoped I would. Or I might embarrass myself. Is that really so bad? Even if I do it and do it badly, it is better than I would have done if I had never attempted it. So I go for it.

You aren't going to die from going after more success, happiness, and prosperity either. Ask yourself, "What's the worst that could happen?" Then go for it. Besides, the worst thing that could happen rarely happens anyway.

SEPTEMBER
13

Read labels. Cut down on fat, salt, calories, and products that contain ingredients you can't pronounce.

SEPTEMBER
14

Failure means little in the grand scheme of things.

It certainly doesn't mean you are a failure; it only means you failed at this one attempt, this time.

Keep going, and you may make history.

SEPTEMBER
15

Turn off the television.

Vow to go just a few hours with it off. Calm down; it's only a few hours! It's hard to be distracted by a black screen. You might think you are going to go crazy, but I promise you won't. You might end up doing some work, or exercising, or having a conversation, or even—dare I suggest—reading a book.

SEPTEMBER
16

Know your kid's friends

and have them over to your house. It's better to have a house full of rowdy kids than to be wondering where your child is.

SEPTEMBER
17

Don't make a jackass of yourself at your kid's sporting events. Being too much of a fan is embarrassing to them, to yourself, and to all of those watching you. This means don't be obnoxious to the other team, to the coaches, or to other parents or officials.

SEPTEMBER
18

When in doubt, wear black. **Black is always appropriate.** It makes you look richer, classier, and best of all, slimmer.

By the way, women have known this for years and never shared this helpful little bit of information with men. They never told us if we put it in black it would look smaller. (That's why I don't have any black underwear.)

SEPTEMBER 19

Here is an easy plan for changing your results: Do anything that's different from the way you have been doing it.

Look at that line again, because it's that important: **Do anything that's different** from the way you have been doing it.

I mean anything. If your life isn't going the way you want it to go, any change will be a positive change. Any change in your actions will lead to a change in your results.

SEPTEMBER 20

Education is effective only **when people want to learn.**

People want to learn most when the stakes are highest and they have a lot to lose by not learning.

SEPTEMBER
21

When you mess up, **it is important not to wallow in your misery for very long.** Lick your wounds, but get over it all pretty quickly. You have to move on.

This concept is equally important when it comes to your successes. Don't wallow in your successes either. Too many people experience a success and then sit back on their laurels (or their butts) and celebrate their successes too much.

The best time to get started on a new project is when you are high on the victory of your last project.

SEPTEMBER
22

You can't teach people how to do the right thing until you teach them how to stop doing the wrong thing. They won't know it is the wrong thing until they see the negative consequences of their behavior. When they become aware of the negative consequences and understand that their own actions created those consequences, then they will begin to understand what the wrong action is and be more willing to change.

SEPTEMBER
23

Focus on what you need to do right now.

Too much time is spent worrying about what happened in the past or fretting about what might happen in the future. The past is just that: passed. It has passed you by and is over, so move on. The future probably isn't going to be as bad as you imagine it to be.

Focus on the present.
It's all you've really got to work with.

SEPTEMBER
24

Action is like a ball rolling downhill. **The momentum builds.** As you get started, one action will lead to another, and that action will lead to another, and before you even realize it, you will have accomplished something significant.

SEPTEMBER
25

Learning to take responsibility for everything you are, everything you do, and everything you have is the biggest challenge you will ever face in your life. Until you first accomplish this major step, it will do you no good to go any further on your quest for success.

SEPTEMBER 26

Regardless of how much you study, how much you learn, and how much you already know, chances are you believe you still don't know enough to reach your goal. You are right. **You don't know everything** you need to know to reach your goal. However, you know enough to start. That's all you really have to know—just enough to start.

SEPTEMBER 27

Your kids are going to want to dress in a way that you think is weird. They are going to have strange hair. They are just trying to discover themselves and be unique. Don't worry about it too much. Green hair grows out. They will abandon their weirdness as they grow out of it— and remember, **they will grow out of it.**

SEPTEMBER
28

To begin a journey and not make it is forgivable.

**Not to begin the jour-
ney at all** is unforgivable.

SEPTEMBER 29

When you ignore bad behavior in your dog, your child, your employee, or others, you are condoning that bad behavior. That makes you guilty by association.

If you and I go out one evening, and you decide to rob someone while I am standing there next to you, and I don't do anything to stop you, a court would find me guilty by association. In my court, if you tolerate or ignore bad behavior in others, you are just as guilty as they are.

If you let your dog bite me, you are going to be the one who pays the consequences. If your kid breaks my window by throwing a rock through it, you will be the one who pays the fine and replaces the window. If your employee treats me badly, you will pay the price by losing me as a customer. Ultimately, you will pay the price because you are responsible for your world. You should control your world.

SEPTEMBER
30

I am a great customer. If you treat me well, I'll tell everyone I know. If you treat me badly, I will tell you, ask for your manager, be specific about what was wrong, and point out how you could have treated me better. (This also makes me a great customer.) After hearing what I have to say, if you apologize, try to make amends, and thank me for pointing out the problem, then I will move on with no hard feelings. I may not come back and give you another shot at my business, but I might. However, if you are rude or apathetic about my feedback, then I will also tell everyone I know.

You should do the same. When you get bad service, **point it out.** When you get great service, **tell people!**

OCTOBER
1

We have become a nation of spectators.

It's easier to watch *Friends* on television than it is to be a friend in real life. It's easier to watch people lose weight on television than it is to get off your huge butt and lose it yourself. It's certainly easier to watch people paint a room or clean out their closets than it is to do it yourself. It's even easier to watch a television nanny correct some other bad parent's out-of-control children than it is to discipline your own.

Most people settle for much less than they have to because they are just too lazy to work for what they really want. They do a half-assed job when they are on the job, and then put little effort into living their dream when they go home. Life, happiness, prosperity, and success all take effort. If it feels easy, you are going in the wrong direction. Stop watching your world drift by; become involved. Success takes effort.

OCTOBER
2

I hate company birth-day parties. You circle up in the break room around some stupid cake, plaster a big fake smile on your face, and sing "Happy Birthday" to someone, knowing your life would be better off if that person had never been born!

By the way, today is my birthday . . . everyone, hold hands and sing along!

OCTOBER
3

The **more** skin you have, the **less** of it the rest of us need or want to see.

OCTOBER
4

If you grow up in a house where your family doesn't work and expects to be taken care of by the government instead of getting a job and working for a living, then you probably won't spend much time working. Instead, you will spend your days watching the mailbox, waiting for your check. That's how we end up with fifth-generation welfare recipients.

If you grow up in a house where people have a **strong work ethic** and a **sense of integrity,** and **pay their bills on time,** then chances are good that you will be that kind of person as well.

OCTOBER
5

Stop being neutral. **Have an opinion. Take a stand.** Be vocal about it. Especially when it comes to raising your kids. Your kids are counting on your guidance. They need to hear what you have to say about life, religion, sex, drugs, money, and other important things. Encourage them to discover others' opinions on all these subjects too. Then talk to them about why you believe what you believe.

OCTOBER
6

Never cut anyone any slack. You earn slack.

OCTOBER
7

The person who doesn't care who gets the credit is a person who has never gotten any credit because his or her contribution has never been worth the credit. Once you have gotten the credit for giving outstanding performance, you will never say it doesn't matter.

OCTOBER
8

"One bad apple can spoil the whole barrel." That is certainly true when it comes to employees. But remember this as well: The whole barrel can't save one bad apple either. **Never sacrifice the whole barrel in favor of the one bad apple.** The only way to deal with the bad apple is to throw it away.

OCTOBER
9

Nothing is more disappointing than finding out you are excellent at doing something that doesn't need to be done at all.

OCTOBER
10

Motivation doesn't work.

You can threaten, coerce, praise, promise, and dangle money, time off, and other carrots of every size, shape, and color, and it will always come down to this: People do what they do when they want to do it and when the consequences of not doing it are painful enough to force them to do it.

OCTOBER
11

Your kids are your fault.

They exist because of what you did. The way they turn out is your fault. If they are fat, it's your fault. If they are lazy, it's your fault. If they don't study, it's your fault. You have control over them. They belong to you and are your total responsibility. You are the adult and your child is the child. You are the leader and the manager and the boss. Keep that chain of command in mind. You must set the example for your kids to follow.

The next time you wonder why your kids are the way they are, here's a clue: Look in the mirror. Your kids always reflect the behavior you have shown them to be acceptable. Your kids are little versions of you.

OCTOBER
12

The speed of the leader

determines the speed of the pack. That rule applies whether you are running a dogsled team, a business, or a family.

OCTOBER
13

Americans arrogantly say they want honesty and integrity from their government officials, yet 20 percent of them cheat on their taxes. Hypocritical? You think? People lie. Millions of Americans lied about how much money they made so they could qualify for a house they knew they couldn't afford and had no business buying. Then they couldn't afford to keep the house and blamed the predatory lenders or the economy. It was not the economy or the lender that got them in trouble; it was the lie. Our politicians lie, and we reelect them. We reward their lies with another term.

Lying is running rampant through our society at all levels. When a guy says he will be there at noon and at three P.M. hasn't shown up, he is a liar. If you let him get away with it, you reward him for his lie. When your daughter says she will be home from her date at ten P.M. according to the curfew you set and she isn't, sorry, but your little princess lied to you, and she is a liar. If you don't enforce any consequences, then you are rewarding her lie. When you allow people to lie to you and don't enforce any consequences, then you are as guilty as they are. When you lie, expect and accept the consequences.

$$$$$$$$$$$$$$

OCTOBER
14

Money makes the world go round. You can argue against that, but it won't matter. You can talk about the evil and corruption that money brings, but I don't care. Money does more good than harm. Money feeds people and builds hospitals. Money builds churches. It even builds the churches for those pious, small-minded people who belittle the rest of the world for focusing too much on money.

I was the guest on a radio show where I was being interviewed about debt. A guy called in and told me that while my ideas were good, I had left out Jesus. I said, "What?" He said, "As long as you keep your hand in the hand of Jesus, you will be fine." I asked him if he was in trouble financially or behind on his credit-card

$$$$$$$$$$$$$

payments. His answer was "Yes." I said, "When you reached for your credit card last time you were at the mall, I guess you had to let go of Jesus's hand to do it, didn't you? Let's not involve Jesus in your stupidity! Jesus didn't make you spend more money than you earn. Jesus doesn't get the blame for that one. You did that all on your own!" Let one of these good folks get in trouble financially because they spent more than they should have or bought too much house or can't make their payments, and they want Jesus to bail them out. Drop to your knees and beg God to help you out of your financial problems! Oh, yeah, that makes sense. I consider that a huge insult to God.

While I have no idea what God would say or even if she would say anything, I would speculate (and hope) that God might say, "You got yourself in this mess, and you can get yourself out of this mess."

OCTOBER
15

Of all the people you think will never leave
you, **you** are the only one.

OCTOBER
16

I have only two prejudices: stupid and fat. Those are my only two because those two are choices. Don't argue with me; they are choices. **Stupidity is a choice:** Read a book! As for fat: Don't whine about your glandular problems, because they just aren't the cause! Fewer than one out of a thousand can even remotely use that as an excuse. And don't blame your genes. Chances are that you haven't fit in your jeans for years! People are fat by choice. Period.

Did you ever eat anything by accident? No, you chose to eat it. No one held a gun to your head. You went to the store, put it in your basket, paid for it, cooked it, and stuffed your face with it. You went to the restaurant and chose it from the menu and paid to eat it. Your choices made you fat— nothing else.

OCTOBER
17

Teamwork doesn't work,
because someone on the team won't work.

OCTOBER
18

When you have an employee, you have the responsibility to both monitor and enforce your position about that employee's behavior. If you don't like your employee's behavior, you should address it and work on that behavior until you get it the way you want it to be. After all, you are paying for it. If you can't fix the behavior, I think you should fire the employee so he or she can go someplace where the behavior fits the job better than it did for you.

But I want you to make sure that it is about the behavior. It is not about the employee. If you don't like the person, that is not part of the deal; you aren't paying for personality. You are paying for that person's results . . . period. Manage and judge the worth of an employee based on results—not personality.

OCTOBER
19

When your kid messes up (and he or she will), don't attack the kid. Simply attack the kid's behavior, as you would with everyone else in your family. Good people do stupid, idiotic things. **Attack the action, the behavior, or the results, but not the person.**

OCTOBER
20

At the drive-in bank: Have your stuff ready before you get there. Don't you dare pull up and then start filling out your paperwork after you get in line, or worse, while you are sitting at the window. You are holding up the line and making the rest of us wait because you are too rude and insensitive to take care of your business before you get to the window! I am sick of getting stuck behind bozos who think that the rest of us have nothing better to do than wait on their sorry butts. It's rude!

OCTOBER
21

Go forth and get even.

When you receive good service, tell people about it. Say thank you to the person who delivered the good service, and then make contact with the manager to point out the great service you received.

When you receive bad service, be polite about it, but don't fail to bring it to someone's attention. Be specific. Don't be rude, get mad, cuss, or lose your temper. Don't be a wimp about it either. Be strong and state your case. Just tell the person what went wrong and explain what you expected by comparison. If the guilty parties apologize and try to make amends, then be gracious, accept the apology, and move on. Realize that maybe this was the exception and not the rule. Then decide to either give them another chance or not.

If the response you get is rude and no one apologizes or tries to make amends in any way, get even by telling everyone you know. If the offense is serious enough, contact the Better Business Bureau. Do what you can to get back at them for expecting you to pay for bad service. Be fair but get even. Stand up for yourself and help the rest of us by doing your part to demand good service from everyone you share your money with. Please don't wimp out and let it slide. The only way customer service will improve is if enough of us refuse to accept bad service. As long as people stay "sheeple" and accept bad service without pointing it out, then bad service will continue. If we all become unwilling to accept anything but good service, then good service is what we will all get.

By the way, when a customer complains about the service you give, remember this concept as well. Say thanks, apologize, and make amends. Ask for another chance to provide good service.

OCTOBER
22

**Focus on accomplish-
ment.** Be known as the person who
gets things done.

OCTOBER
23

It is not up to the school system to make sure your kid gets an education—**it's up to you.** You have to make sure that your kids grow up knowing how to speak well, add and subtract, and handle money. It's up to you to teach them about life, sex, relationships, how to get along with others, and how to be successful. Don't pawn off the education of your child to the school system alone. Ultimately, you are responsible.

OCTOBER
24

Don't nag your kids. Don't threaten your kids. Tell them what you expect from them. Explain what the consequences will be for not doing what you told them to do. Then tell them you have confidence in their ability and willingness to do it. If they do what you asked, then give a word of praise and appreciation. If they don't do it, give them one courtesy warning. If it doesn't get done at that point, then execute the consequences. This is how you shape behavior. This is how you set a good example. This is how you build character. This is good parenting.

OCTOBER
25

Superstar employees get to write their own rules because their results earned them that right. Mediocre employees don't get that privilege because they have mediocre results.

OCTOBER
26

Why do you work? I know why I work.
I work for the money.
Period. After a speech I gave recently, the
president of the company approached me
and said how lucky I was to be able to experience my passion like that. I asked him
what he was talking about and he said,
"Your speech. That is your passion; it's ob-
vious." I said, "Thanks, but that speech is
not my passion. That speech is my job. I
am really good at my job and I'm glad you
enjoyed me doing my job, but what you
just witnessed is anything but my passion.
I enjoy it, but I'm not passionate about
giving speeches."

He was incredulous. I told him my passion was my wife, my boys, my bulldogs,
and my free time. I told him I was passion-

ate about sitting on my back patio with a glass of fine scotch in my left hand, a great cigar in my right hand, my bulldog Ralph on my lap, and my wife by my side, watching the sun go down over the mountain while Merle Haggard plays in the background. That is something I can get passionate about. The rest is work. I do what I do for the money. I do what I do to pay for the life I love. I do what I do to finance as many nights sitting on my patio as I can get. That is why I work. How about you?

OCTOBER
27

You can't get rich keeping other people broke. **Share the wealth.**

OCTOBER
28

One of my favorite John Wayne movies is *The Shootist*. In it, Wayne's character, J. B. Books, has a code by which he lives: "I won't be wronged. I won't be insulted. And I won't be laid a hand on. I don't do these things to other people and I require the same from them."

I love that code. It's clear. It's manly. It's honorable. It's reciprocal. It's fair.

Mine is: I will do my best to be authentic in all that I do. I will treat others fairly based on their actions. I will be giving with all that I have. I will love people enough to tell them the truth. I refuse to be lied to or accept abuse at any level.

But I'm adding John Wayne's to mine, I think.

What is your code? Don't have one? That reminds me of the old saying "If you stand for nothing, you will fall for anything."

OCTOBER
29

Teenagers. God love 'em. I say that because there are times when I am sure that only God could possibly love them. I once told my teenage son Tyler that I loved him but couldn't stand him. Been there? Here is a word of encouragement: They grow out of it. Thank God!

OCTOBER
30

Do what you know is the right thing to do. Don't kid yourself; you always know the right thing to do. The right thing to do is rarely the easy thing to do.

OCTOBER
31

What do you want them to say about you when you die? That you were a real go-getter? A workaholic? Always made your quota? A mean SOB? A gossip? You may be saying that you don't care because you will be dead. I get that. But I still care what people will say about me when I'm gone. I would love for my boys to say I was a great dad. I want my wife to be able to say that I loved her and she never doubted it. I want my friends to say I was fun, honest, open, and clear. Based on that, I try to live that way. **How will you be remembered?**

NOVEMBER
1

Nip it in the bud! Remember that line by Barney Fife from *The Andy Griffith Show*? Barney was passing out parenting advice to Andy about correcting a behavior of Opie's. He told Andy, "Nip it in the bud. Nip it!" The point was a good one then and still is: When you see bad behavior, nip it in the bud.

I was reminded of this recently while watching Cesar Millan, the Dog Whisperer. In the segment I am referring to, a big dog had food aggression. The owners could not go near the dog or the food bowl, as the dog would growl, bark, and nip at them. They had not done much to correct the problem, and Cesar was quick to point out that since the behavior had not been corrected early in the dog's development, the aggressive behavior was now spreading to other areas beyond the food. He said that if the aggression was not brought under control quickly and firmly, it wouldn't be long before that dog was going to hurt someone. Then he took control and taught the dog owners how to take control. That's his position: You are in charge of your environment and your dog—take control!

This is great advice. **Correct problems when you see them** so they don't spread and grow. Take control of your environment.

These are good ideas when dealing with dogs and children. We have all seen children who have been allowed to get away with things that should have been corrected. We all know that the bad behavior will spread and that the ill-behaved child will become bigger and bigger until, like in the case of the dog, someone is going to get hurt.

Nip it in the bud.

NOVEMBER
2

Your children will accept and emulate the values you show them. If you value honesty, integrity, and keeping your word, and you expect those things in all of your dealings with them and with others, then you will have kids who value honesty and integrity and keeping their word. **Decide the values that you want your children to have,** and then demonstrate those values through your own behavior.

$$$$$$$$$$$$$$$

NOVEMBER
3

I just saw a commercial for mattresses. They want you to finance your mattress for five years. If you have to finance your mattress, you should probably sleep on the floor!

Which leads me to another rant. Have you seen the commercial where the couple goes to a fine restaurant and orders a meal and the meal is so small that afterward they stop by a convenience store to load up on Twinkies, chips, and soft drinks so they can fill up? Then they charge it? Of course, it's a credit-card commercial. Listen, if you have to charge your soft drinks and treats, you shouldn't be at the fine restaurant to begin with. Of course, you shouldn't be buying the treats on credit either!

$$$$$$$$$$$$$$$

NOVEMBER
4

Americans are idiots when it comes to food. Not because of what we eat but because of how much we eat. I am as guilty as anyone. I eat stuff that is bad for me. I could also afford to lose ten pounds and be much better off. Don't think I am standing on my soapbox preaching what I don't need to hear myself. I *love* food. I love food that is bad for me. I love biscuits and gravy and chicken-fried steak and all things greasy. I *could* eat these things at every meal and be happy. Instead, I try to eat them just every once in a while to remind me of my roots and satisfy my grease cravings. Even then, I try *not* to clean my plate but to eat just enough to get full. Try that yourself—**eat until you are full,** then push the plate away. Ask the waiter to take the plate. Even if you had only two bites, if you are full, stop eating!

NOVEMBER 5

Five things my dad taught me:

1. Smile; it don't cost nothing. (Bad grammar, good lesson.)
2. Two ears, one mouth: Listen twice as much as you talk.
3. When a man hires you to work, you work. He's the boss, and you do what he says whether you like it or not. That's how you get paid.
4. When you give your word, you keep it, no matter what. A man is only as good as his word.
5. Look people in the eye when you talk to them.

What lessons did you learn from your parents? What lessons are you teaching your child?

NOVEMBER
6

I watched a woman on the *Today* show talk about her latest book on the importance of telling the truth in various situations. When asked why people lie, she said, "Lying is such an ugly word; let's call it editing the truth." Editing the truth? Are you kidding me? Let's not call it what it is, and then we won't hurt anyone's feelings. Let's put lipstick on the pig one more time! Let's dress it up and make it look pretty instead of calling it what it really is. That's the problem. When you don't confront people with their lies, the result is that they don't think they have done anything wrong. Unless you call people liars for lying, they might not think they have actually lied— they might think they have just edited the truth. Bottom line: We have a nation of people who either don't know they are doing wrong or don't care. Either way, they lack integrity.

NOVEMBER
7

Why do people do what they do? I get that question often. **Do you ever wonder why people do what they do?** There are three answers to the question. First, people do what they do because they want to do it. Second, people do what they do because the consequences for not doing it are not painful enough to keep them from doing it. Third, people do what they do because they think they won't get caught.

NOVEMBER
8

People say they want a great relationship
with their spouse or significant other, yet
a recent study said that 65 percent of people spend more time with their computer
than with their spouse. Why is that? Is it
because their computer gives them more
companionship? Or better sex? Ouch! I
actually said that! Most people make very
little effort to look good or smell good or
have a conversation with their spouse.
They crawl into bed with bad breath,
smelling like a goat, and then gripe about
the fact that their spouse doesn't want to
have sex with them.

NOVEMBER
9

People say they want job security, they
want a promotion, they want to be respected
at work, or they want a raise. Yet they show
up late and put in minimum effort. Most of
them do just enough work so they won't get
fired. Yet, they can't figure out why they
aren't doing better.

NOVEMBER
10

I am amazed at how many people don't seem to have mastered basic skills like grammar and spelling. I regularly get e-mails from people who must have typed them with their elbows. No one could have hit that many wrong keys with their fingers! Do people not have a spell-checker? Come on. When you type a word and your computer highlights it in red, that is a clue that it might need some attention.

Pet peeves of mine:

"your" instead of "you're" and "there" instead of "their." A spell-checker probably won't catch these, but you should be smart enough to know the difference!

NOVEMBER
11

To have a goal and not accomplish it is forgivable.

Not to have a goal at all is unforgivable.

NOVEMBER
12

Don't think your journey in any area is going to be all smooth sailing. It won't be. **You are going to make mistakes.** You are going to slip up. You are going to experience setbacks. You are going to fall off the wagon. You are going to fail from time to time. Welcome to the real world. It happens. Dust yourself off and start again! Regroup. Refocus. Don't whine. Think about what went wrong and why it went wrong. Then suck it up and get back to work!

NOVEMBER
13

Affirmation without implementation is self-delusion. What does that mean? **Saying positive words isn't enough.** You have to prove you are ready to change your life by taking action on the words!

NOVEMBER
14

Refuse to become involved in anything that does not move you closer to accomplishing your goals. This is challenging, but you have to stay tough. Ask yourself this question: Does this activity move me closer to where I want to be or farther away from where I want to be? Answer yourself honestly, then do only the things that move you closer to where you want to be in your life.

$$$$$$$$$$$$$$$

NOVEMBER
15

If your outgo exceeds your income, then your upkeep becomes your downfall.

$$$$$$$$$$$$$$$

NOVEMBER
16

On average, people spend twenty hours per week watching television and less than two hours per week reading. Fifty-eight percent of Americans won't read a nonfiction book after high school. Forty-two percent of university graduates never read another book after college. Only 20 percent will buy or read a book this year. Seventy percent have not been in a library or bookstore in the past five years. I guess these folks think they have all the information necessary to be successful, prosperous, happy, and healthy.

NOVEMBER 17

When it comes to dealing with your children, remember that you aren't perfect, so don't pretend to be. Admit your mistakes. If you overcorrect, punish unfairly, or yell when you shouldn't, stop and admit it to your child. Apologize. Parents who create personas that are always right and never make a mistake will lose their credibility and the respect of their children very quickly.

NOVEMBER
18

Don't make your problems into disasters. Deal with every problem the way it really is, not the way you imagine it is or could get. The worst thing that could happen rarely does happen. Write your problem on a sheet of paper and deal with the reality of your problem and not what you imagine it to be.

NOVEMBER
19

Want to be happier? **Give up the constant need to be right.** This one is a huge issue for me. I like to be right. I don't think I am alone with this one; I believe all of us enjoy being right. What kind of idiot enjoys being wrong? Pick your battles. Not everything is a battle. Sometimes, it really isn't worth the fight even when you know you are right and can win.

NOVEMBER
20

Remember that everything that happens to you causes you to grow in some way— even the lousy stuff. In fact, especially the lousy stuff. **Be thankful for the lesson** even when you find it hard to be thankful for the lousy stuff that caused it.

NOVEMBER
21

Every time you start to feel sorry for
yourself and think that your life sucks,
watch an episode of *The Jerry Springer
Show*. **Those people's lives
really suck!** You aren't nearly as
bad off as you think you are!

NOVEMBER 22

There was a television commercial many years ago where everyone in the world had to sign their work. The street sweeper, the guy who mowed the lawn—everyone had to sign their work, taking credit for what they had accomplished. That commercial was about **pride in workmanship,** something that is certainly lacking in society today.

We should all work as though we are going to have to sign our name to everything we do. I bet the quality of workmanship would improve quite a bit if we knew that everyone around us would be giving us the credit or the blame for all that we do.

NOVEMBER
23

Good advice on dealing with your spouse or kids: **Hug more. Gripe less.**

This is a short, simple lesson that can reap big results. If it won't matter tomorrow, then let it go today. Hug it out!

NOVEMBER
24

Don't put your kids in front of your marriage. Don't put so much effort into raising your kids that you end up neglecting your spouse. Raising kids is the most important thing you will ever do in your life. I get that. You owe them your very best. But there will come a time when the kids will be grown and will go away and you will be left looking at that person you married. Make sure that person isn't a stranger.

NOVEMBER 25

What happened to the work ethic of our parents? They worked because they took their commitments and their obligations seriously. They had been raised to believe that your word is your bond and that when you tell someone you will work, then you work—with no argument. If someone hurt your feelings, oh, well, that was part of the job. If you got hurt, oh, well, at least you had a job. If someone made you mad, again, that was part of the job. If you worked with idiots, you dealt with it. If your boss was a jerk, you put up with it—she was the boss.

"But, Larry, haven't we come a long way in terms of employees' rights since then?" What about the company's rights? What about the rights of the customer? The employee has the right to do the job he or she was hired to do for the wage that was agreed upon. The employee has the right to a physically safe environment. That's about it. No workplace is stress free. No job is a picnic. **It's called work for a reason!**

$$$$$$$$$$$$$$

NOVEMBER
26

If it sounds too good to be true, it is. Don't fall victim to scams that sound too good to resist. There is not a prince in Nigeria who has $10 million being held in an account, who needs two grand from you to get it released, and who will split it with you if you will help him. People actually fall for this stuff. Why? We like to believe that there is something other than work that is going to make us rich.

$$$$$$$$$$$$$$

NOVEMBER
27

Be careful what you wear out in public. Before you run out the door in the pair of sweats with the baggy butt and the hole in the knee, think about how you would feel if you bumped into your best customer. It's embarrassing to be dressed like a slob and have someone say, "Aren't you that guy on TV?" Trust me on that one!

NOVEMBER
28

When you are going out with your significant other, do him or her a favor before you walk out the door and try a little honesty. I am amazed when I see couples out and she looks great—heels, little black dress, jewelry, the works—and he looks like he just got back from wrestling a goat. Ladies, say something! **Don't go out with this bozo until he cleans up** and puts on his big-boy pants and some real shoes!

NOVEMBER
29

You can't win every argument. Sometimes you are going to lose. It happens. When it does, don't be an ass about it. Besides, you deserve to lose about half the arguments you get into. Why? Because you are wrong. There are other arguments you get into that you never should have gotten into to begin with. It doesn't matter if you win those or not. **Win the ones that count.**

NOVEMBER 30

I hear people say that they want to age gracefully. Why would you want to do that? Go out kicking and screaming. **Old age is for sissies!** Stay fit, stay fun, and kick ass 'til you die.

I agree with Cher. When asked what was good about growing old, she said, "Not a damn thing!" My feelings exactly.

DECEMBER
1

Why should you care about becoming as successful as you possibly can? **Because you can.** Those three words are the key. Make as much money as you can, become as healthy as you can, be as happy as you can, be as good at your job as you can. Be as successful in every area of your life as you possibly can. Why? Because you can. You are obligated to become as much as you can be simply because you can!

$$$$$$$$$$$$$$$

DECEMBER
2

When I was a little boy my dad taught me a very valuable lesson about money. He said, "You can't borrow or spend your way out of debt." I asked him, "Then how do you get out of debt?" He replied, "You work hard and pay your way out." That lesson has served me well for many years. I think it would serve our government and many businesses well too. I think it is a lesson our entire society needs to learn. When you find yourself in debt, don't think that spending or borrowing will fix your situation. Instead, go to work and start paying your way out.

$$$$$$$$$$$$$$

DECEMBER
3

Lighten up. Don't get your panties in a wad. Most of the stuff you are upset about isn't going to matter in the long run. In fact, most of it won't matter in a half hour.

DECEMBER
4

He that walketh with wise men shall be wise.

PROVERBS 13:20

He that walketh with a dumbass shall also be known as a dumbass.

LARRY'S PROVERBS 1:08

DECEMBER
5

Scope up! Give up pettiness on all levels.

Does it really matter if the toothpaste tube gets squeezed from the middle or from the end?

At a restaurant, who cares who had dessert and who didn't? Just split the check and move on.

Don't be petty—it is so unattractive.

DECEMBER
6

Forget blame. You can either fix the blame or fix the problem. Spend your time fixing the problem. I get caught up in this one from time to time myself. I like to point the finger of blame. I am good at it. I know how to make a case to figure out whose fault it is better than just about anyone else. After I've put energy into blaming someone, I actually feel a little better . . . temporarily. However, I am still no closer to getting past the problem and on to the solution. I have found it better to skip the blaming part and just head straight toward the solution.

DECEMBER 7

When I am not getting the results I want, I try to become aware of why that is happening. Every time, it is because I have done something stupid. I have acted in a way that is inconsistent with my words and my wants. **No exception— it is always my fault.** By the way, this applies to you and your results too. When you are not getting what you want, it is because you are doing something stupid.

DECEMBER
8

Sales success in a nut-shell:

Find out what people want and give them more of it. Find out what people don't want, and then don't give them any of that. How do you find out what people want and don't want? Ask them. It's amazing what you can find out if you only ask.

DECEMBER
9

Most customers will gladly pay more for
less when they have confidence that they
will be served well in the process.

DECEMBER
10

When evaluating people and their job performance, ask yourself these two things:

Does the employee have the **desire** to do the job?

Does the employee have the **ability** to do the job?

What you will find most often is that employees have the ability to do the job but no desire to do the job. That's too bad because you can teach the ability but you can't do a damn thing about desire.

DECEMBER
11

You have a reputation. You might be known as a good guy. That certainly is not a bad thing. You might be known as a good guy who can't really be counted on. That isn't a good thing. You got that reputation because of your past actions. **If you want a good reputation,** then you have to be aware of your actions. Sometimes, your reputation will slam the door in your face long before you ever arrive.

DECEMBER
12

When dealing with jerks, remember this: Never lower yourself to their level. That's where they want you. Instead, you can really tick them off by rising above them and the situation they have put you in. When they get mad, either ignore them or laugh in their faces, but don't argue with them. Remember: They invented the game, and when you sink to their level to play it with them, they win.

DECEMBER
13

Sometimes the light at the end of the tunnel is a train. Every cloud does not have a silver lining. Sometimes it is hiding a tornado. All problems are not opportunities. Hey, Mr. Positive—back off. Wipe that stupid smile off your face, take your rose-colored glasses off, and get a grip on reality. Things are crap and it is going to take a realistic view and some hard work to fix them!

DECEMBER
14

Sometimes you will not love or even enjoy your work. Sometimes it will suck and you will hate it. That's when you remember the deal you made when you were hired: that you would show up and work. That deal was not conditional on you loving your job or feeling good or enjoying yourself. Your coworkers, customers, and company shouldn't have to suffer just because today you aren't having fun at what you do. **Suck it up and go back to work.**

DECEMBER
15

If your business sucks,

it is because as a businessperson, you suck.

If your sales suck, it is because as a salesperson, you suck.

If your employees suck, it is because as a manager, you suck.

If your customer service sucks, it is because you deliver sucky customer service.

Everything in your life sucks because you suck.

DECEMBER
16

The ultimate boss in any business is the customer.

We all have customers, though we call them by different names. Attorneys call them clients. Doctors call them patients. Authors call them readers. Speakers call them the audience. Most businesses just call them customers. It doesn't really matter what you call them, but it is important to know that the customer is your boss. Customers have the money, and you are there to serve them well in order to get them to share that money with you. They decide whether you will survive during tough times and how much you will flourish during good times. Customers also get to tell you whether you are doing your job well and to complain if you aren't. You work for the customers—the most important entities in any business.

DECEMBER
17

You shouldn't have to work too hard on your friendships. **Friendships should be easy.** If you have to work hard to maintain the friendship, then it isn't much of a friendship. Friends accept you and let you be the way you are. They allow you to have good days and bad days. They let you be an idiot and make an ass of yourself. They even let you whine. But a real friend won't let you do any of this for very long. A real friend will also tell you that you are being stupid and that you need to do better.

DECEMBER
18

Answer this: What is more important: what you do or what you get done? Easy answer: What you get done is the most important. **Throw away your to-do lists** and get yourself some what-I-have-to-get-done lists.

DECEMBER
19

Why is there always enough time to do it over and never enough time to do it right the first time?

DECEMBER
20

Clean up the clutter. Take some time to go through your closet and clean out the clothes you haven't worn this year. Go through those junk drawers in your kitchen and clean them out. Go to your garage and get rid of some of the junk you have been tripping over to get to your car. Go through your desk drawers and get rid of the stuff you no longer absolutely have to have to get your job done. Take the time to simplify your life by getting rid of all the things that clutter up your life.

DECEMBER
21

What's the most important thing in a marriage? It's not love. Love in a long-term day-to-day relationship is totally overrated. It's a bonus. I love lots of people. But I don't like very many people. There are lots of times when my wife and I have a hard time loving each other. She's pretty lovable, but me? Not so much. However, there has never been one time, regardless of what we were going through, when I didn't like her more than anyone else on the planet. I like being with her and spending time with her and talking to her more than any other person. I would rather share a meal, a movie, an experience, or a joke with her than with anyone else. That's why it works for us. That's why she puts up with me, and that's why I put up with her. We genuinely like each other. That has little to do with our marriage. It has to do with two people who have chosen to be with each other through the best of times, but more important through the worst of times, simply because we like each other so much. The fact that we love each other most of the time is purely a bonus.

DECEMBER
22

The ability **to forgive people is hard,** probably because we don't think other people deserve forgiveness. And they probably don't. Seriously. They probably don't deserve to be forgiven and didn't even ask for forgiveness. So get over forgiving people because they deserve it. You should forgive people because you deserve it, not because they deserve it. You deserve to move past the injustice. You deserve to get on with your life and past the hurt. Remember that you deserve the very best that life has to offer, and the only way to experience that is to forgive others so you can be happy.

DECEMBER
23

One of the most important things I remember reading was "Your cup of joy can only be as deep as your cup of sorrow." I argued with that idea for a long time. I didn't want to think that in order for me to enjoy the good that I had to experience the bad. In fact, I deeply resented the concept. I am older and somewhat wiser now and have experienced much more than when I first considered this idea. I have had more mountaintop experiences and spent more time in the valleys.

This is what I have learned: **The valley is a place of learning.** It is a place of rest. It's where you experience humility. It is where you get to know the authentic you. It is where you rebuild your energy so you can start back up the mountain again. Mountaintops are exhilarating and fun to conquer. But it is hard to stay up there unless you sit down or set up camp. When you do that you become lazy and stagnant, and someone will eventually show up and kick you off the mountain. It is best to enjoy your time on top, but understand that every up has a down. All highs have a low. The key is **to enjoy them both.**

DECEMBER 24

How do you know when you have made it? If you are alive, you haven't. You never realize your ultimate potential. You never make all the money you can make. You never learn all the lessons there are to be learned. You never serve as many people as you can serve. You never give as much as you can give. You never work as hard as you can work. You never love as much as you can love, and you certainly never have as much fun as you can have.

Don't think of "making it" in terms of achievement. Instead, know that you are in the constant state of making it if you are doing all you can do in every area of your life until the day you die. It's not about getting there; it's about the trip.

DECEMBER
25

This day is a reminder of giving—not receiving, but **giving.** As I get older I realize that life is not so much about what you get but about what you give away. I am a very selfish giver. While that may not make sense to you, I can assure you it's true. I like the way I feel when I give someone something just because I know they would enjoy it. I like the buzz I get from giving because I can afford to. I like the feeling I get when I have given to the point of sacrifice, whether it's in terms of time, money, or service. I selfishly give because I like what it does for me. Others may benefit from my gifts, but I am the big winner.

Giving is also the best insurance policy I know. If you want to make sure you always have good things coming to you, then make sure you are always giving away some of the good you have.

DECEMBER
26

If life is no fun, it is because you are no fun. Your life is always a reflection of who you are. Fun people lead fun lives. Don't argue with me—deal with it. Become more fun. Get friends who are more fun. Buy a joke book. Watch some funny movies. Look in the mirror and laugh at yourself. **Try this:** Stop taking things, including yourself, so seriously. Life is not as complicated as you have made it out to be.

DECEMBER 27

The **cold, hard truth.** Did you hear that?

That's why people don't like the truth—because **it isn't warm and fuzzy;** it's cold and hard. That's why they say, "The truth hurts." In fact, that's how you know it's the truth.

DECEMBER
28

Sex is the coolest thing on the planet, yet our society does everything it can to make it wrong or dirty. We try to legislate it, limit it, and decide whom it's okay to have sex with and not have sex with. None of that works. In fact, the result is that people just want to do it more. So what is the answer? More sex. Do it as much as you can with someone you love until the day you die. If you are lucky, that's how you will die. If this offends you, it's because you aren't getting any.

So as long as everyone is of age and consenting, get after it! **Sex is meant to be enjoyed.** We came equipped to do it and are meant to do it. It is the physical expression of our feelings toward another person. Sometimes it's just plain fun to do for no other reason than that.

Sexual expression rarely causes societal problems. Sexual repression almost always does.

$$$$$$$$$$$$

DECEMBER
29

Productivity sucks. Want me to prove it?
**What have you accom-
plished today?** Seriously. What
have you done that actually contributes to
the bottom line of the organization that
writes you a check? Don't lie. Now, cut
that answer by about 75 percent and you
will be closer to the real truth about what
you have actually accomplished.

$$$$$$$$$$$$

DECEMBER
30

Get a sheet of paper and write down exactly what you want your life to look like. Be detailed. Then focus on these things every day. Add to the list when you think of something. This is not goal setting—this is priority setting. Your thoughts, your words, and your actions always go toward what is important to you. If the things you wrote down are indeed your priorities, then take action today. Then you really can be happy, healthy, successful, and rich.

DECEMBER
31

If you knew for sure that one idea could make you $1 million, when would be a good time to get started on it? How about next year? Does that sound like a good time to start working on that idea?

If you're broke right now and you could really use the money, why don't you wait a year until you are more in the mood or more inspired or motivated to get started? That makes sense, doesn't it?

Good ideas don't get better with time. When you discover a great idea that can change your life for the better, do something about it right now!

LARRY WINGET

The Pitbull of Personal Development®

www.larrywinget.com

OTHER BOOKS BY LARRY WINGET

People Are Idiots and I Can Prove It!: The 10 Ways You Are Sabotaging Yourself and How You Can Overcome Them; Gotham Books 2009

You're Broke Because You Want to Be: How to Stop Getting By and Start Getting Ahead; Gotham Books 2008

It's Called Work for a Reason!: Your Success Is Your Own Damn Fault; Gotham Books 2007

Shut Up, Stop Whining, and Get a Life: A Kick-Butt Approach to a Better Life; Wiley 2004

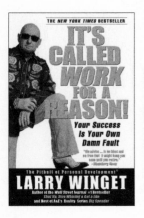
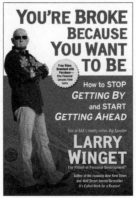
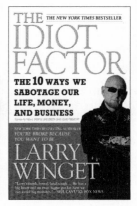

And coming from Gotham in winter 2010, *The Idiot Factor* in paperback and Larry's new book on parenting, *Your Kids Are Your Own Fault.*